Dorothy E Zemach Carlos Islam

Writing in Paragraphs

from sentence to paragraph

MACMILLAN

Contents

To the Teacher

Writing is an important form of communication in day-to-day life, but it is especially important in secondary school and university. Writing is also one of the most difficult skills to master in both a first language and a second language. Students can find it challenging to find ideas to include in their writing, and each culture has its own style for organising academic writing. However, with the help of this book and your guidance, your students will learn to recognise good academic paragraphs and develop their own paragraph writing skills.

Writing in Paragraphs is designed to help low-intermediate students analyse model paragraphs, find ideas for their writing, put their ideas into sentences, organise their sentences into paragraphs, review their paragraphs, and revise their paragraphs so that they become even stronger. This process approach to writing will not only develop your students' paragraph writing skills, but will also encourage them to become independent and creative writers.

Each main unit provides an interesting theme to engage your students and motivate them to read and analyse the model paragraphs. The unit themes also inspire your students to create their own writing. An introductory unit looks at how students can format their writing and introduces the idea of process writing.

The activities in each unit help students with a particular aspect of paragraph writing, such as brainstorming, writing topic sentences, and developing paragraphs with supporting sentences. A unit's activities might also teach correct punctuation for academic writing and useful grammatical functions for writing, such as conjunctions and transition expressions. The units also show students how to review their own and their classmates' writing in order to make revisions.

Each unit ends with a structured writing assignment that provides an opportunity for students to use everything presented in the unit. Included in this book are samples of a paragraph from brainstorming to final draft, with a completed Peer Review Form. There is also a guide to common grammatical terms and concepts useful for writers, a list of irregular verbs and their past tense forms and participles, and a guide to punctuation. Finally, there is an answer key with answers to most of the exercises and a photocopiable section with blank Peer Review Forms and a Writing Survey you may like to do with your students at the start of the course.

Learning to write well takes a lot of practice and patience. Students need clear guidance, positive feedback, and interesting ideas to write about. We hope this book provides this for you and you enjoy using it.

To the Student

Writing is a very important part of your school and university study. You will write assignments that may be one paragraph or several paragraphs, and you will write answers for tests and exams that may be a few sentences, a paragraph or two, or a complete essay.

Academic writing in English may be different not only from academic writing in your own language, but even from other writing in English. The purpose of this book is to help you recognise and produce the sort of paragraph writing that will be expected of you in academic situations.

During this course, you will have many opportunities to study and discuss examples of English academic paragraph writing. You will also have many opportunities to discuss your own paragraphs and the paragraphs of your classmates. You will learn how important the reader is to the writer, and how to express clearly and directly what you mean to communicate. We hope that what you learn in this course will help you throughout your academic studies and beyond.

You should come to your writing class every day with energy and a willingness to work and learn. Your teacher and your classmates have much to share with you, and you have much to share with them. By coming to class with your questions, taking chances and trying new ways, and expressing your ideas in another language, you will add not only to your own world, but to the world of those around you. Good luck!

Introduction

In this unit, you will learn ...
- **formatting for assignments.**
- **how to write headings.**
- **about process writing.**

Layout/Formatting

1a Match the words about layout with their definitions.

a. paragraph
b. margin
c. double line spacing
d. indent (v)
e. title
f. font

1. To start a paragraph further in from the edge of the page than the rest of the text.
2. The space at the side of the page where nothing is written.
3. A set of letters in one size and style used for printing and computer documents.
4. A section of a piece of writing that starts on a new line and contains several sentences.
5. The name of a piece of writing.
6. A style of spacing where there are two blank lines between each line of text.

There are no set rules about how you set out your paragraphs and they can be hand written or word-processed. It is down to personal preference whether you use indentation, double line spacing or a certain font, unless your school or university has specific requirements. However, the general rule is that paragraphs should be clearly visible, easily readable and in one font, which is usually black.

1b Look at these student papers. Tick (✓) the one that is better for an academic assignment.

a. ☐

School uniforms are not good for students. They are not attractive, so students feel bad when they are wearing them. Students like to express their personalities by choosing their own clothes.

b. ☐

School uniforms are not good for students. They are not attractive, so students feel bad when they are wearing them. Students like to express their personalities by choosing their own clothes.

2 **Look at these different ways of writing headings for student papers. Answer the questions below.**

a.

Karen Chou
Professor Miller
English Writing 1
12 April, 2004

School Uniforms Are Good

1. What is the writer's name?
2. What is the name of the class?
3. Who is teaching the class?
4. What is the title of the assignment?

b.

Sebastian Mitchell
School uniforms
2nd draft
5 September, 2004

Students Should Choose Their Own Clothes

1. What is the writer's name?
2. What is the title of the assignment?
3. What is the assignment about?
4. What does '2nd draft' mean?
5. When did the writer write the assignment?

How does your teacher want you to write headings in this class?
Write an example here:

Process writing

3 **Take a quiz! First guess the correct answers. Then read the paragraphs below to check your guesses.**

a. 'Process writing' means

- ☐ writing in English.
- ☐ writing with a word processor.
- ☐ writing in several stages (steps).

b. Before you begin to write, you should

- ☐ finish the homework for your other classes.
- ☐ get some ideas.
- ☐ ask your friends for help.

c. Your teacher may ask you to read a classmate's paper and answer some questions about it. This is because

- ☐ you can learn a lot by reading your classmate's assignment.
- ☐ your teacher is too busy to read all the students' papers.
- ☐ you are a better writer than your classmate.

d. Your teacher may ask you to write another draft. This is because

- ☐ your teacher can't think of any new assignments.
- ☐ the first time, your paper was bad.
- ☐ you can make your paper better by making some changes.

e. Before you hand in your paper for a grade, you should

- ☐ ask your teacher to give you a good grade.
- ☐ check it carefully.
- ☐ put some pretty stickers on it.

a. Musicians practise their pieces many times before a concert. Athletes work out before a competition. In the same way, good writers go through several stages when they write. 'Process writing' will guide you through these stages so your final paper is really your best effort.

b. The first stage of process writing is getting ideas. In this course, you will learn and practise several different ways to get ideas. Try them all and see which way works best for you.

c. An important stage in process writing is sharing your writing. You can see how other writers like you handled the same assignment, and you can get some good ideas from them. You can also see how well someone else understands your ideas.

d. After you finish your assignment, put it away for some time. When you look at it again, you may have new ideas. Your classmates may help you find new ideas, too. Writing your paper again (called 'revising') gives you the chance to improve your paper.

e. Before you give your teacher your paper, check it carefully. Read it aloud. Does it sound natural? Did you forget any words? Did you remember to write the heading correctly? Does your paper look neat? Remember to give your teacher your best effort!

1 Beginning to Work

In this unit, you will ...
- recognise and write complete sentences.
- learn how to begin and end a sentence.
- learn the common features of a paragraph.
- identify the topic of a paragraph.
- identify strong and weak paragraphs.

1 Look at this chart. Tick (✓) the answers for your country.

	It's common.	It's not common.	I'm not sure. / It depends.
a. Secondary school students have part-time jobs.	☐	☐	☐
b. University students have part-time jobs.	☐	☐	☐
c. University students have volunteer jobs (jobs that don't pay a salary).	☐	☐	☐
d. Part-time jobs pay a good salary.	☐	☐	☐
e. After graduation, both men and women want to find a full-time job.	☐	☐	☐

2 Share your information with a group of your classmates. Ask and answer these questions about part-time jobs.

- What are common part-time jobs?
- Have you ever had a job? What was your first job?
- What kind of job do you think is best for a secondary school / university student?
- (your idea)

3 **You are going to read a paragraph called *Part-time Jobs and Secondary School*. What do you think the paragraph is about? Circle the answer.**

a. Useful secondary school subjects
b. Working and studying at the same time
c. How much money a part-time job pays

4 **Read the paragraph. Did you choose the right answer in exercise 3 above?**

Part-time Jobs and Secondary School

1. Secondary school students should not have part-time jobs. 2. Secondary school is a very important time for a student, and students are very busy. 3. Students have to study hard to enter a good university. 4. Many secondary school students also play sports, and they practise before and after school. 5. Secondary school students also spend time with friends of the same age. 6. Those friendships can be important for the rest of their lives. 7. A part-time job takes time away from studying, playing sports, and making friends. 8. People work for most of their adult lives. 9. When they are in school, it's important for them to just be students.

5 **Which sentence tells the writer's most important idea?**

1 ☐ 2 ☐ 3 ☐ 8 ☐

6 **What do sentences 3, 4 and 5 do?**

a. They show new ideas.
b. They give examples.
c. They show different opinions.

7 **Do you agree with the writer? Why / Why not?**

Writing focus: What is a sentence?

How many words are in the shortest English sentence? Except for one-word commands (*Sit!*), a complete sentence in English needs two words: a subject (a noun or pronoun) and a predicate (a verb) (*She sits*).

Of course, most English sentences are longer than just two words, but every sentence tells a complete thought. Groups of words that do not make complete sentences are called *phrases*.

If you need more information on complete sentences and phrases, see pages 86–88.

8 Work with a partner. Look at the following. Some of them could be sentences with the correct punctuation. Tick (✓) the ones that could be sentences.

a. ☐ after school
b. ☐ we love writing in English
c. ☐ his friends are not in his class
d. ☐ the man in the striped suit
e. ☐ at three o'clock in the afternoon
f. ☐ graduated in May
g. ☐ is going shopping this weekend

Language focus: Capital letters and final punctuation

Sentences in a paragraph …

- start with a capital letter
  Part-time jobs can be stressful.
- end with a full stop (.) question mark (?) or exclamation mark (!)
  Many students work as tutors.
  How old were you when you got your first job?
  I will never work in a restaurant again!

Note: Exclamation marks are not as common in academic writing as they are in casual writing. Don't use them too often. Never use more than one exclamation mark at the end of a sentence in academic writing.
The company offered me a part-time job!! = when writing to friends
The company offered me a part-time job. = when writing in school

9 **Unscramble the sentences and write them on the lines below. Begin and end each sentence correctly.**

a. in a shop / my sister / works

My sister works in a shop.

b. is / a useful subject / computer science

....

c. don't / I / like / working with people

....

d. can't find / many students / a job / easily

....

e. more women / are / after university / working ?

....

f. first job / was / my / wonderful / a / experience

....

10 **Look again at exercise 8 on page 7. Write the complete sentences with correct punctuation. Add to the phrases to make complete sentences. Then share your sentences with a partner. How are they different?**

a. ....

b. ....

c. ....

d. ....

e. ....

f. ....

g. ....

Writing focus: What is a paragraph?

A paragraph is a group of about 6–12 sentences about one *topic*. Every sentence in a strong paragraph is about the same topic. All of the sentences explain the writer's *main idea* (most important idea) about that topic. When the writer wants to write about a new main idea, he / she begins a new paragraph.

A paragraph can give information, tell an opinion, explain something, or even tell a short story. The sentences are arranged logically, so the reader can easily understand what the writer wants to say.

In academic writing, a paragraph has a *topic sentence* that directly tells the reader the main idea. The other sentences in the paragraph, called *supporting sentences*, give more information about the topic. They add specific details and explanations. In academic English, the topic sentence is usually (but not always!) first or last.

1 Work with a partner. Read the groups of sentences below and on page 10. Circle the letters of the strong paragraphs. If you think the sentences make a weak paragraph, say why. Choose one or more of these reasons:

- The sentences are not all about the same topic.
- There are not enough sentences.
- There is no topic sentence.
- Some sentences say the same thing.

When I need a good place to study, I go to the library. It's always quiet there, so I can concentrate. It's easy to find the books I need, and I can search for information on the Internet because there are several computers. The other people in the library are also reading or working, so the mood is good for studying. I study better and faster in the library than in any other place.

a. ....

....

I need to buy a motorbike. With a motorbike, I could get to my job more quickly. It takes two hours to get to work by train. That's very slow. A motorbike is much faster. If I had a motorbike, I could save a lot of time. Taking the train is not fast enough for me.

b. ....

....

First, insert a blank CD into the computer. Then, select the song list that you want to copy. You will see a button that says, 'Click here to burn.' Click on that button. Then just wait a few minutes. That's all!

c. ....

....

I will never forget my first day of secondary school. I was very nervous because I didn't know any of the other students. In my first class, I looked around for someone friendly. I saw a girl at the front of the room who also looked nervous, so I decided to make friends with her. Even though I was shy about talking to her, I went up to her and said, 'Don't be nervous. I will help you. Do you want to sit with me?' She looked a little surprised and said, 'Actually, I am the new teacher.'

d. ....

....

Mobile phones are very popular. They are really convenient. They're small and light.

e. ....

....

Sports instructor is a good part-time job. You can enjoy your favourite activity and earn money at the same time. Some other jobs pay better. You can also volunteer as an instructor. I had a difficult time learning to swim, because my instructor wasn't very good. My tennis instructor was much better. If you get a lot of experience as a sports instructor, you can get a job at a gym or as a coach in the future.

f. ....

....

12 **Read this paragraph about a student's first job. What is the topic?**

a. Working in a laboratory
b. Getting my first job
c. What my first job taught me

Learning Responsibility

1. My first job was as a sales assistant in a small clothes shop. 2. It wasn't a difficult job, and it wasn't really a very interesting job. 3. My best friend had a more exciting job. 4. Every weekend I had to open the shop at 10.00 a.m. 5. I couldn't be late. 6. Now at weekends I like to sleep late. 7. I helped customers find clothes, and I kept the shop clean and tidy. 8. My parents' house was very clean, too. 9. I used the cash register and handled credit cards, so I had to be very careful. 10. These things all taught me responsibility. 11. Now I work in a research laboratory. 12. I don't work with clothes anymore, but I still use that important skill I learnt in my first job.

13 **Cross out the sentences that are not connected to the topic.**

14 **Which additional sentences could be connected to the paragraph? Write C (connected) or U (unconnected).**

a. .... I answered the phone and opened the post.

b. .... On weekdays I did my homework for school.

c. .... I once worked delivering pizza, too.

d. .... I learned how to choose and order new clothing.

e. .... Dressing neatly and professionally was an important part of the job.

f. .... A lab assistant is a good job for me.

g. .... In the future, I would like to take some business trips.

Put it together

15 **Look at these sentences for a paragraph about having a part-time job in secondary school. Cross out the ones that are not connected. On a separate sheet of paper, write a paragraph using the connected sentences. They are already in the right order but are not yet correctly punctuated.**

having a part-time job is a valuable experience for secondary school students

they can learn many things that are not usually taught in a classroom

for example, they can learn how to work with older people

I was the youngest person in my school class

they also get experience with the business world

I took a business class at university that was very good

having a part-time job gives students a sense of independence

they can also earn money to use for university

university tuition in the U.S. is more expensive than in many other countries

education is more than just school subjects

learning about the real world is also important

some universities help their graduates find jobs after graduation

16 **Check your writing.**

Did you ...

- ☐ include a heading on your paper?
- ☐ format the paragraph properly (see page 2)?
- ☐ start and end each sentence correctly?
- ☐ give the paragraph a title?

17 **Hand in your paragraph to your teacher.**

2 *Giving and Receiving Presents*

In this unit, you will ...
- **identify topics and main ideas.**
- **identify strong and weak topic sentences.**
- **practise writing topic sentences.**
- **combine sentences using *and* and *but*.**
- **learn how to use commas in sentences with *and* and *but*.**

1 Tell a partner about the last present you received.

- Who gave you the present?
- When did they give you the present?
- What was the present? Did you like it?

2 Read the paragraph and answer the questions.

a. What is the topic of the paragraph?
  1. celebrating birthdays
  2. the writer's family
  3. choosing presents

b. What is the writer's most important opinion about the topic?
  1. Presents should be old.
  2. Presents should be chosen carefully.
  3. A photograph is a good birthday present.

c. Why does the writer like the photograph?
  1. It helps him think about his father.
  2. It wasn't expensive.
  3. It was a birthday present.

A Birthday Present

1. Choosing a birthday present for a friend or family member is fun, but it can be difficult. 2. The present should be personal and has to be thoughtful. 3. For example, the best birthday present I ever got wasn't fancy or expensive. 4. Last year my mother gave me a photograph of my father when he was my age. 5. He is standing with his mother and father (my grandparents) in front of their house, and he looks happy. 6. I think of my father every time I see that photo. 7. It was a perfect birthday present.

Writing focus: Topic sentences

A good topic sentence should include either of the following:

- one clear topic
  weak: *It's important to have friends, and also to do well in school.*
  strong: *I don't think I will ever have a better friend than Heather.*
- an opinion or idea about the topic
  weak: *I have been studying karate.*
  strong: *Studying karate has given me strength and self-confidence.*

A good topic sentence should **not** be:

- too *broad* (too much to write about)
  weak: *Australia is an interesting country.*
  strong: *On my visit to Australia, I saw many unusual animals.*
- too *narrow* (not enough to write about / is just a fact)
  weak: *School starts at 8.30 a.m.*
  strong: *Getting ready for school in the morning is more difficult than any of my classes.*

Remember
The topic sentence is *usually* the first or last sentence, but it can be any sentence in the paragraph.

3 Look at these topic sentences. Circle the topic of the sentence. Underline the main idea.

a. My sister is my best friend.
b. Snowboarding is my favourite winter sport.
c. The last CD I bought changed my life.
d. There are three reasons why my mobile phone is useful.
e. Reading books, such as the Harry Potter stories, can help students improve their English.
f. My part-time job taught me several new skills.
g. Disneyland was a great place for our family holiday.

4 Look again at the paragraph on page 13, *A Birthday Present*. Which sentence is the topic sentence? Circle the topic and underline the main idea.

5 **In the following pairs, circle the number of the best topic sentence. Then explain your choice to a partner. Say why the sentence you didn't choose is weak. Use one or more of these reasons:**

- It's too broad.
- It's too narrow.
- There is no main idea or opinion.
- There is more than one main idea.

a. **1.** Many people in England and the United States have cats.
(2.) Cats are good company for their owners.
There is no strong opinion or idea about the topic; it is too broad.

b. **1.** Studying English at secondary school helps you get a better job.
2. We study English at secondary school.
....

c. **1.** The food and people in Japan, Taiwan, and Korea are very interesting and different, and so are the buildings.
2. Traditional Japanese food is different from Korean food.
....

d. **1.** My grandfather has helped me in many ways.
2. My grandfather is 86 years old.
....

e. **1.** I really like sports.
2. Rugby has taught me many things about life.
....

f. **1.** There are many environmental problems around the world.
2. It's important to save the rainforests in South America.
....

g. **1.** I got an A on my last maths test.
2. I have a secret technique for learning maths.
....

6 **Improve these topic sentences. Circle the topic. Choose a main idea for each topic and write a topic sentence. Then share your new sentences with a partner or small group.**

a. I have a photo of my girlfriend.

idea: *The photo reminds me of her.*

topic sentence: *I carry a photo of my girlfriend to remind me of her.*

b. I have a new jacket.

idea: ....

topic sentence: ....

c. The Internet is good.

idea: ....

topic sentence: ....

d. My friend is nice.

idea: ....

topic sentence: ....

e. I learn English at school.

idea: ....

topic sentence: ....

Language focus: Using and *and* but *to join sentences*

7 **Work with a partner. Look at these pairs of sentences. How are they similar? How are they different? Which do you like better, and why?**

a. **1.** I sent my mother a birthday card. I called her.
2. I sent my mother a birthday card and called her.

b. **1.** I like getting flowers. I don't like getting chocolates.
2. I like getting flowers, but I don't like getting chocolates.

c. **1.** I didn't send my brother a birthday present. He didn't send me one.
2. I didn't send my brother a birthday present, and he didn't send me one.

- In each case, the sentences in 2 *flow* better – that is, they sound more fluent and natural.
- Sentences about the same topic can often be combined with words like *and* and *but.*
- Use *and* to join *similar* ideas. In 7a, the writer did two things for her mother's birthday (sent a card; called her). How are the actions in 7c similar?
- Use *but* to show *contrasting* ideas: good / bad, easy / difficult, positive / negative. What is the contrast in 7b?

8 **Look again at the paragraph on page 13, *A Birthday Present*. Underline the sentences joined by *and* and *but*.**

9 Complete this paragraph with ***and*** or ***but***.

Same Holiday, Different Customs

People in the United States and Japan celebrate Valentine's Day on 14th February. However, the holiday is celebrated in different ways in each country. In the U.S., Valentine's Day is enjoyed by friends and romantic partners, a. .... in Japan usually only romantic partners celebrate this day. Chocolate is the most popular gift in Japan, b. .... it is common in the U.S. too. However, in the U.S., other kinds of gifts are also given, c. .... many people exchange cards. The biggest difference is that in Japan, girls and women give chocolate to boys and men, d. .... in the U.S., boys and girls give cards or small gifts to all of their friends. American men and women give gifts and cards to each other. In fact, women usually get more expensive gifts than men. I would like to be a man in Japan, e. .... a woman in the U.S.!

Note: Don't begin sentences with *And* or *But* in academic writing. Use *In addition* or *However* instead.

Language focus: Punctuation

When you join two complete sentences with *but*, you must always use a comma before *but*:
I didn't want to send her a present. I sent her one anyway.
I didn't want to send her a present, but I sent her one anyway.

When you join two complete sentences with *and* and the subjects of the sentences are both written, use a comma before *and*:
Shopping in the town centre is expensive. Parking is hard to find.
Shopping in the town centre is expensive, and parking is hard to find.
(*Shopping* and *parking* are both written.)

When you join two complete sentences and remove the subject of the second sentence, don't use a comma before *and*:
These days people post paper cards. People e-mail electronic cards.
These days people post paper cards and e-mail electronic cards.
These days people send paper and electronic cards.
(The subject *people* is not written a second time.)

10 Join these sentences with *and* or *but*. Use a comma if you need one. Then share your sentences with a partner. Did you make the same choices? Talk about any differences.

a. I got a camera for my birthday. I got clothes for Christmas.

I got a camera for my birthday and clothes for Christmas. ....

I got a camera for my birthday, and I got clothes for Christmas. ....

b. Ahmed speaks English very well. He enjoys his classes.

....

c. Yoshi studies hard. He doesn't get good grades.

....

d. In Asia, most people eat rice for breakfast. In Canada, most people have cereal.

....

e. Morocco has lovely mountains. Morocco has beautiful beaches.

....

f. Spanish is spoken in most of South America. Portuguese is spoken in Brazil.

....

g. Presents are difficult to choose. Presents are fun to give.

....

h. Noodles are easy to cook. Noodles are popular in many countries.

....

Put it together

11 **Make a quick list of presents you have given and received.**

Presents given	Presents received
....	....
....	....
....	....
....	....

12 **Choose one present. Tell your partner about it. Ask and answer questions like these.**

Presents given

- Who did you give it to?
- When did you give it?
- Why did you choose this present?
- What did your friend or family member think of the present you gave?
- (your ideas)

Presents received

- Who gave it to you?
- When did you receive it?
- Why did someone choose that present for you?
- What did you think of the present?
- (your ideas)

13 **On a separate sheet of paper, write a topic sentence about your present, and then write sentences with *and* and *but*.**

14 **Exchange papers with a partner.**

- Circle your partner's topic and underline the main idea.
- Circle the commas your partner used.
- Talk with your partner and decide if your commas are in the right places.

15 **Hand in your sentences to your teacher.**

3 A Favourite Place

In this unit, you will ...
- develop paragraphs with descriptive details.
- use lists to brainstorm.
- learn to edit lists.
- combine sentences containing adjectives.
- write about places.

1 Describe this picture to a partner. Have you been to the beach before? Tell your partner what it was like.

2 Read the paragraph and answer the questions on page 21 with a partner.

Relaxing at the Beach

1. Where is your favourite summer holiday place? 2. The beach is the perfect place for me. 3. The air is hot, but the water is cool, wet and fresh. 4. First, I enjoy swimming and surfing in the sea. 5. When I am tired, I come out and lie on the beach. 6. The sand is soft and white. 7. The beach is noisy with seagulls and children laughing, but it's a pleasant noise. 8. I even like the beach smells. 9. The air smells salty from the sea and sweet from everybody's sun cream. 10. I feel peaceful and relaxed. 11. When I want to relax in summer, I go to the beach!

a. Which sentence is the topic sentence?

1 ☐ 2 ☐ 10 ☐

b. What do sentences 3, 4, 6, 7 and 9 do?

1. Say the same information in a different way.
2. Tell a story about the topic.
3. Explain the topic sentence by giving more information.

Language focus: Descriptive vocabulary

You know that a topic sentence tells the main idea of a paragraph. *Supporting sentences* develop the paragraph by adding more information. When you describe a place, you can develop your paragraph by adding descriptive details – information that tells how a place looks, sounds, smells, or feels.

3 **With a partner, put these adjectives that can describe places into the table below. Some words can be used in more than one place. Check a dictionary or ask your teacher to explain any new words.**

dark	friendly	musical	soft
dry	green	quiet	spicy
exciting	humid	relaxed	sweet
fragrant	loud	sharp	warm

look	sound	smell	feel
....	....	....	....
....	....	....	....
....	....	....	....
....	....	....	....
....	....	....	....
....	....	....	....
....	....	....	....
....	....	....	....

4 **Look again at the paragraph on page 20, *Relaxing at the Beach*. Circle the descriptive adjectives, and then put them into the table in exercise 3 above.**

3

Brainstorming: Lists

You cannot write if you don't have something to write about. So, before they start to write, good writers *brainstorm* ideas (they think of and write down ideas that they can use).

In this book, you will practise several different ways of brainstorming. Try them all, and then choose the way that works best for you.

How to make a list

- Use a separate, whole sheet of paper.
- Write your topic at the top.
- Write down as many ideas as you can about your topic.
- Write single words or short phrases, but don't write long sentences.
- Write down every idea that comes to you, and don't worry about whether the ideas are 'good' or 'bad'.

Editing your list

After you brainstorm, you need to go back and see which ideas you can use. This is called *editing*.

- Underline or highlight the good ideas.
- Cross out ideas that are not related to your topic or that you don't want to use.

5 **This example shows a list for the paragraph on page 20, *Relaxing at the Beach*. Cross out the ideas that the writer didn't use. Compare your list with a partner, and say why you think the writer didn't use the crossed out ideas.**

Beach

holiday
relax
air – hot, dry, windy?
water – cold, cool, fresh, wet
swim, surf
can't windsurf
seagulls
good snack food
beach umbrellas / expensive to rent
too far away
smell – salt, sun cream
feel – sand
sounds – birds, children, ocean waves
taste – salt water tastes bad

6 **Choose one of the topics below. In five minutes, make a list of ideas. Share your list with a partner. How many descriptive adjectives did your partner use?**

a. My favourite place to relax
b. An interesting city

7 **Edit your list by crossing out unrelated ideas or ones you don't like. Show your partner what you crossed out, and explain your decisions.**

Writing focus: Combining sentences containing adjectives

8 **Look at the picture. With a partner, brainstorm a list of adjectives to describe the scene.**

9 **Read the following paragraphs. How are they the same? How are they different? Which paragraph seems better to you? Explain your choice to a partner. Then check your ideas below.**

My Mother's Kitchen

1. My mother's kitchen is not big. 2. It is comfortable. 3. It is warm. 4. My mother cooks a lot. 5. Her kitchen smells spicy. 6. It smells sweet. 7. Sometimes she taught my brother and me how to cook. 8. We liked learning new things. 9. We liked working together. 10. We liked making delicious foods. 11. Now I live far away. 12. I often think about my mother's kitchen.

My Mother's Kitchen

1. My mother's kitchen is not big, but it is warm and comfortable. 2. My mother cooks a lot, and her kitchen smells spicy and sweet. 3. Sometimes she taught my brother and me how to cook. 4. We liked learning new things, working together, and making delicious foods. 5. Now I live far away, but I often think about my mother's kitchen.

The first paragraph is less interesting because many sentences are all the same type: noun + verb + adjective.

You remember from Unit 2 that sentences about similar topics can often be combined. One effective way to do this is by combining sentences with adjectives.

To make more varied and interesting sentences, you can:

- combine the adjectives in two sentences with *and* or *but*. Remove the subject and verb from the second sentence.

  Example: *The film was long. The film was boring.*

  and
  The film was long~~. The film was~~ boring.
  The film was long and boring.

  Example: *Our homework is difficult. Our homework is fun to do.*

  , but
  Our homework is difficult~~. Our homework is~~ fun to do.
  Our homework is difficult, but fun to do.

- combine three sentences. Notice how a comma is used between the first two adjectives. Remove the subjects and verbs from the second and third sentences.

  Example: *Her skirt was short. It was black. It was fashionable.*

  , and
  Her skirt was short~~. It was~~ black~~. It was~~ fashionable.
  Her skirt was short, black and fashionable.

10 **Find and underline three examples of combined sentences in the paragraph on page 20, *Relaxing at the Beach*.**

11 **Combine these sentences. Then compare with a partner. Which sentences did you combine the same way? Which were different?**

a. Charles is interesting. He is a little strange.

....

b. The river was deep. The river was wide. It was cold.

....

c. Our teacher is strict. He is fair.

....

d. July was hot. It was humid.

....

e. Kim is my best friend because she is kind. She is smart. She is funny.

....

f. The food in that restaurant is delicious. It is expensive.

....

Put it together

12 **Work with a partner to complete the paragraph below and make it better. First, make a list of details you could add to the paragraph. This is an imaginary place, so use your imagination!**

A Horrible Hotel

....

The rooms are small. The rooms are dark. The rooms are dirty. There is no air-conditioning. The rooms are hot in summer. There is no heating. The rooms are cold in winter. There are big windows. The view is terrible. ....

....

....

....

....

That is why I want to warn you never to stay in this hotel.

13 **On a separate sheet of paper, write your completed paragraph.**

- Combine sentences to make it more interesting.
- Write a topic sentence.

14 **Check your writing.**

Did you ...

☐ include a heading on your paper?

☐ format the paragraph properly (see page 2)?

☐ start and end each sentence correctly?

15 **Exchange papers with another pair. Compare your paragraphs. What is the same? What is different? Which do you like the best?**

16 **Hand in your paragraph to your teacher.**

4 An Exceptional Person

In this unit you will ...

- **use word maps to brainstorm.**
- **practise using adjectives in sentences.**
- **learn to write concluding sentences.**
- **learn when to use capital letters.**
- **write about people.**

1 **Look at the people and describe them to a partner.**

2 **Read this paragraph about Jack Collins. Decide which person is most like Jack. Then answer the questions on page 27.**

Jack Collins

1. Jack Collins is the most amazing person I have ever met. 2. He came to my school and talked about his difficult life in prison. 3. He was in prison for 15 years. 4. He made a lot of mistakes when he was young, but now he has changed his life. 5. He saw a lot of violence in prison, so he uses his experience to help secondary school students. 6. Jack is tall and strong. 7. He also looks a little scary because he has some spider tattoos. 8. The thing I remember most is his sensitive personality. 9. He really wants to help young people. 10. I've never met anyone like Jack before.

a. Which sentence is the topic sentence?
Circle the topic and underline the main idea.
b. Which sentences tell about Jack's personality?
c. Which sentences tell about Jack's physical appearance?

3 **Find the nouns these adjectives describe:**

a. amazing	person..................	**d.** tall, strong	....
b. difficult	....	**e.** scary	....
c. young	....	**f.** sensitive	....

Note: Nouns can be used as adjectives; for example, ***spider*** *tattoos* in the paragraph on page 26 about Jack Collins.

4 **Look again at the paragraph on page 26, *Jack Collins*, and underline the other noun that has been used as an adjective.**

Brainstorming: Word maps

Remember
In Unit 3, you learned that brainstorming was used ...
- to think of many ideas for your writing.
- to help you see the connections between ideas.

and you learned how to brainstorm using lists.

A word map is another kind of brainstorming. Word maps can help you think of many ideas for your writing and see the connections between the ideas.

- Use a separate, whole sheet of paper.
- Write your topic in the middle, and draw a circle around it.
- Write an idea about the topic nearby, and circle it.
- Draw a line to connect the circles. This shows that the idea and the topic are related.
- Add more ideas and circle the ideas.
- Draw lines to connect any circles with related ideas.
- Write down as many ideas as you can. Don't worry about whether they are 'good' or 'bad'.
- After you finish, cross out any ideas you don't want to use.

This example shows a word map for the paragraph on page 26, *Jack Collins*. Notice which ideas the writer kept and which ones he / she crossed out.

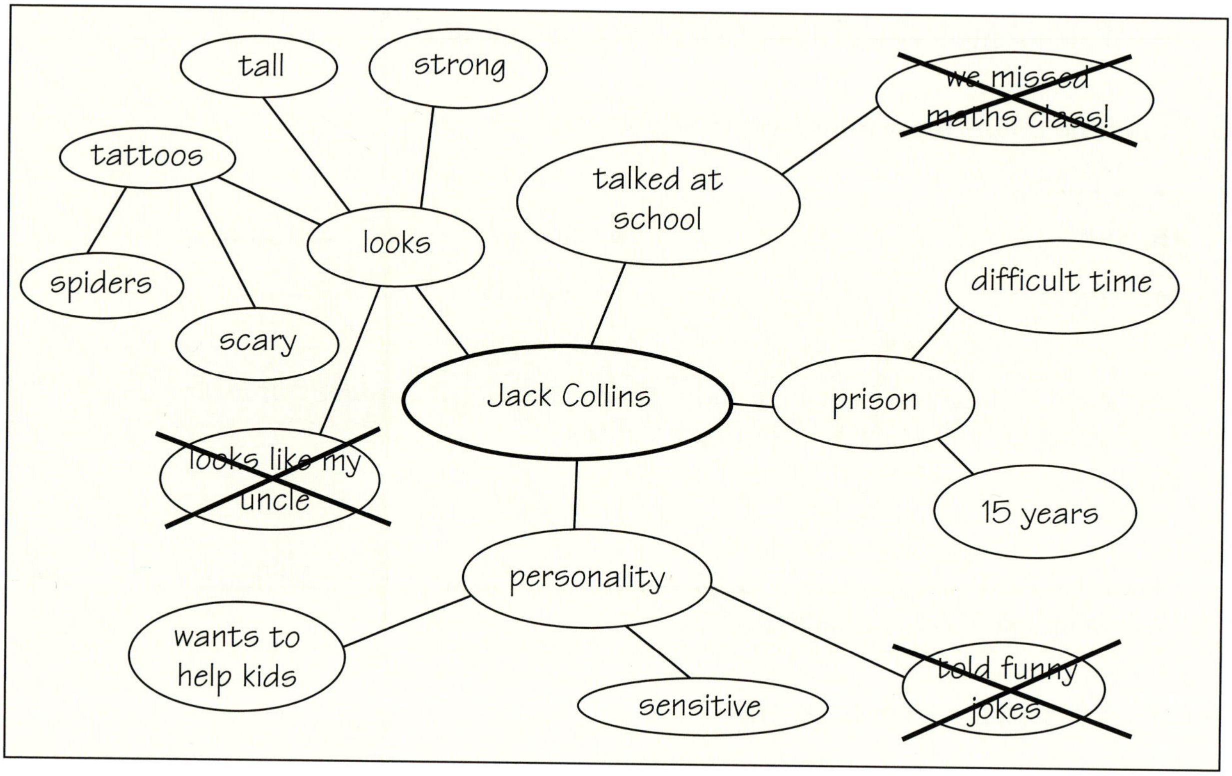

5 **On a separate sheet of paper, make a word map for one of the topics below.**

- Use plenty of descriptive adjectives.
- Share your word map with a partner.
- How many descriptive adjectives did your partner use?

a. A relative
b. A teacher who helped me
c. A film / music star

Language focus: Using adjectives in sentences

Adjectives can be used in three different ways:

- before a noun
  Jack Collins is the most **amazing person** *I have ever met.*
- after a form of the *be* verb
  He made a lot of mistakes when **he was young**.
- after a verb like *taste, sound, look, feel, smell, seem*
  He also **looks a little scary**.

6 **Write sentences with each descriptive adjective that you used in your word map. Try to write all three different types of sentence.**

7 **Look at the pictures and do the following.**

a. Write two or three adjectives for each person on a separate sheet of paper. You can write adjectives for their physical appearance or their personality (use your imagination!).

b. Exchange papers with a partner. Write sentences using your partner's adjectives. Then share your sentences.

Writing focus: Concluding sentences

A good paragraph has a clear topic sentence and supporting sentences that explain and support the topic sentence. Many (but not all) paragraphs also have a concluding sentence. The concluding sentence closes the paragraph.

A concluding sentence can ...

- restate the topic sentence.
- summarise the main idea of the paragraph.
- make a prediction connected to the paragraph's topic.
- make a suggestion or give advice connected to the topic.

A concluding sentence **does not** state a completely new idea.

8 **Read these concluding sentences for the paragraph on page 26, *Jack Collins*, and decide if they 1 (restate), 2 (summarise), 3 (predict) or 4 (suggest or advise).**

a. .... I've never met anyone like Jack before.

b. .... I think Jack will help many teenagers stay out of prison.

c. .... Everyone should talk to someone who has been to prison.

d. .... Jack's experiences, appearance, and personality make him very memorable.

9 **The paragraph below is called *My Best Friend's Grandfather*. With a partner, think of three or four things the paragraph could be about.**

10 **Read the paragraph and find out if any of your guesses were correct.**

My Best Friend's Grandfather

1. We can all learn from listening to our grandparents. 2. My best friend's grandfather tells great stories about his life. 3. He's 94 years old, but his voice is still strong and clear. 4. He speaks quietly and slowly when he tells stories. 5. His life was difficult when he was young. 6. His family didn't have much money, and he worked hard. 7. Even though his life was not easy, he is positive and optimistic. 8. I can learn many things from his stories.

....

....

....

11 **Read the sentences below and do the following.**

a. Decide which sentence could not be a concluding sentence for the paragraph *My Best Friend's Grandfather.*
b. Put the sentence you like best into the paragraph.
c. Tell a partner which concluding sentence you chose and why.

1. My best friend's grandfather is a wonderful storyteller.
2. My best friend's grandfather is a good example for me.
3. My best friend's grandfather never went to university.
4. I think all teenagers should listen to their grandparents' stories.

12 Look at the picture of the football player, David Beckham, and describe him to a partner.

13 Write a concluding sentence for the paragraph, *A Popular Athlete*, about David Beckham. Share your sentence with other students. Decide whether the sentences restate, summarise, predict, or suggest / advise.

A Popular Athlete

1. David Beckham became a famous football player in the late 1990s, and by 2003 was the most recognisable athlete in the world. 2. He was a popular player first in England for Manchester United and then in Spain for Real Madrid. 3. They are both successful and very rich football teams. 4. Beckham is a valuable player because he can take dangerous free kicks and pass the ball long distances. Beckham is not only a talented player but also a fantastic leader. He led his country, England, in the 2002 World Cup where they only lost to Brazil. His fans also respect him because he is a very hard worker on the field and on the training ground.

....

....

....

Language focus: Punctuation

Capitalisation

Remember
In Unit 1, you learned that the first word of a sentence starts with a capital letter.

A word is also capitalised if it is ...

- in the title of a piece of writing (paragraph, essay, book), a film, a piece of music, etc. **Don't** capitalise prepositions (*of, to, with*), articles (*a, the*), or conjunctions (*and, but*).
- a name of a group, a place, or a person; that is, a *proper noun*.
- a day of the week or a month.
- a language or a nationality.

Note: A *proper noun* is the name of a specific person, place, or thing. For example, *Picasso* is the name of a specific person, *Paris* is the name of a specific place, *the Olympics* is the name of a specific thing.

14 **Find all of the capitalised words in the paragraph on page 31, *A Popular Athlete*. Tell a partner why each word is capitalised.**

15 **Rewrite the following sentences using correct capitalisation.**

a. david beckham married victoria adams, who was a singer with the spice girls, a pop group in the 1990s.

....

b. beckham learned to speak spanish because he moved to madrid.

....

c. in march 1999, david and victoria had their first son.

....

d. the beckhams now have three children, called brooklyn, romeo and cruz.

....

e. romeo was born in september 2002 and cruz was born in February 2005.

....

f. there is a funny film called 'bend it like beckham,' which is about one of david beckham's fans.

....

Put it together

16 **With a partner, match the topic sentence on the left to the concluding sentence on the right.**

a. .... I admire many things about my father.

b. .... I think my uncle's face shows his personality.

c. .... Daniel Radcliffe, who plays Harry Potter, is my favourite actor.

d. .... I was always frightened of my history teacher.

e. .... My mother is a very busy person.

f. .... Elvis' body and health changed as he got older.

1. You can easily see that he is friendly, outgoing, and loves to laugh.
2. She works hard at her job, but she always has time for me.
3. His poor health is probably why he died young.
4. When I grow up, I hope I will be just like my father.
5. She was scary, but I learned a lot from her tough lessons and strict personality!
6. I think he will keep improving as he gets older and makes more films.

17 **Choose one of the pairs of sentences in exercise 16 above. Make a word map about the topic. Use your imagination!**

18 **Look at a partner's map and say which ideas are most interesting to you.**

19 **On a separate sheet of paper, write a paragraph.**

- Write the topic sentence and concluding sentence you chose in 17.
- Add supporting sentences by using the details from your word map.

20 **Check your writing.**

Did you ...

☐ include a heading on your paper?

☐ format the paragraph correctly?

☐ start and end each sentence correctly?

☐ give the paragraph a title?

21 **Exchange papers with a partner. Talk with your partner and decide if all the supporting sentences are related to the idea in the topic sentence.**

22 **Hand in your paragraph to your teacher.**

5 Trends and Fashions

In this unit, you will ...

- **review descriptive vocabulary.**
- **use freewriting to brainstorm.**
- **review what a paragraph contains.**
- **develop peer feedback skills.**
- **write a paragraph about a trend.**

1 **Talk with a partner or small group. In many Western countries, it has become popular for young people to get tattoos. Is this true in your country? Do you know anyone with a tattoo? Would you ever get one?**

2 **Why do people get tattoos? With your group or partner, make a list of all the reasons you can think of. Then read this paragraph to see if any of your reasons were mentioned.**

Beautiful Forever!

1. My friends think I'm crazy. 2. My father says I'll never get a job now, and my mother is worried that I won't get married. 3. However, I'm glad I got a tattoo. 4. Last month, I had a beautiful sun design tattooed onto the top of my left arm. 5. It's smallish, neat and feminine. 6. It won't get lost like jewellery or wear out like clothing. 7. Even when I am old, I will still have my lovely sun. 8. It makes me feel unique and confident. 9. I know some people think tattoos are unattractive, but I love the special look of my new symbol.

3 **Read the paragraph on page 34, *Beautiful Forever!*, again and answer these questions.**

a. Which sentence is the topic sentence?

1 ☐ 2 ☐ 3 ☐ 7 ☐

b. What do sentences 5, 6 and 8 do?

1. Say the same information in a different way.
2. Tell a story about the topic.
3. Explain the topic sentence by giving more information.

c. Which of these sentences could be added to the paragraph?

1. It was designed by a famous artist.
2. Chinese characters are popular for tattoos these days.
3. My father doesn't like pierced ears, either.
4. Even when I wear clothing that covers my tattoo, I feel special because I know it's there.

Language focus: Vocabulary review

4 **Work with a partner. Look at these adjectives from Units 1–4. Do they describe people, places, or things? Write the words in the appropriate column. You can use some words in more than one column. Then add two more words of your own to each column.**

busy	convenient	comfortable
difficult	exciting	friendly
humid	noisy	peaceful
optimistic	popular	salty
shy	spicy	valuable

people	places	things
....	....	....
....	....	....
....	....	....
....	....	....
....	....	....
....	....	....
....	....	....
....	....	....

Brainstorming: Freewriting

Freewriting is a kind of brainstorming where you write everything you can think of, quickly and without stopping. Freewriting helps to improve your writing fluency, and gives you ideas for your writing.

- Write as much as possible for five or ten minutes.
- Don't worry about spelling, grammar, or punctuation.
- If you make a mistake, just cross it out and continue writing.
- Write continuously, without stopping.

Remember that when you make a list or a word map, you write words or short phrases. When you freewrite, you write sentences.

Look at this example of freewriting on the topic of trends and fashions.

What is trendy or fashionable now? I can't think of anything. Do I have anything that is fashionable? I don't think so. Everyone has a mobile phone now. But mobile phones aren't very interesting. What is fashionable these days? What about ~~teliviss~~ TV? Reality TV is fashionable. There are a lot of reality TV shows these days. 'The Apprentice' is pretty good. There are 14 normal people who have to live together. These people work in teams and have to complete business tasks. Every week one candidate on the losing team is fired. At the end, Alan Sugar picks a winner from the last two people, and they win a £100,000 job with him. I wish I had £100,000! 'Big Brother' is terrible. Some people live in a house and every week there is a vote and one person leaves. It is similar to 'The Apprentice' but ~~bowling~~ boring. These people are not allowed to leave the house. They don't have very much to do and they often have arguments and fights. I think most people who go on reality TV are a little strange.

5 **Choose one of these topics. For five minutes, write as much as you can on a separate sheet of paper. Write everything that comes into your mind, without stopping.**

a. A clothing trend
b. A trend I don't like
c. A popular item I own (or would like to own!)

Editing your freewriting
After you freewrite, you need to edit what you have written – go back and see which ideas you can use. It is useful to:

- underline the good ideas.
- cross out anything you don't want to use.

6 **Look at the edited freewriting below. What topic do you think the writer will use for his / her paragraph? Why did the writer cross out or underline some sentences? Explain to a partner. Use reasons like these:**

- The sentence wasn't about the topic.
- The sentence wasn't interesting.
- The sentence was interesting.

What is trendy or fashionable now? ~~I can't think of anything. Do I have anything that is fashionable? I don't' think so. Everyone has a mobile phone now. But mobile phones aren't very interesting. What is fashionable these days? What about telivis TV?~~ Reality TV is fashionable. There are a lot of reality TV shows these days. 'The Apprentice' is pretty good. There are 14 normal people who have to live together. These people work in teams and have to complete business tasks. Every week one candidate on the losing team is fired. At the end, Alan Sugar picks a winner from the last two people, and they win a £100,000 job with him. ~~I wish I had £100,000!~~ 'Big Brother' is terrible. Some people live in a house and every week there is a vote and one person leaves. It is similar to 'The Apprentice' but ~~bowling~~ boring. These people are not allowed to leave the house. They don't have very much to do and they often have arguments and fights. I think most people who go on reality TV are a little strange.

7 **Look at your freewriting from exercise 5 on page 36. Underline sentences that you think are interesting or useful. Cross out anything that is not useful.**

8 **Spend another five minutes freewriting, starting with a sentence or phrase you have underlined.**

9 **Look at your two examples of freewriting together. Do you have enough ideas for a paragraph? If not, freewrite some more!**

Paragraph review

Remember
A paragraph can contain three different types of sentence:
- A **topic sentence** – tells the reader the topic and main idea of the paragraph.
- **Supporting sentences** – develop, explain and give details about the idea of the topic.
- A **concluding sentence** – restates the topic sentence, summarises the paragraph, makes a prediction, or gives advice or suggestions.

10 **Below are sentences from a paragraph in the wrong order. Decide if the sentences are topic sentences (T), supporting sentences (S), or concluding sentences (C).**

a. .... So, I bought a bike last week for £150 in a second-hand bike sale.

b. .... The colors are bright red, white and dark blue.

c. .... It's a great bike and I'm going to have a lot of fun on it.

d. .... Mountain bikes are really popular where I live. Everybody has one.

e. .... The bike is one year old but looks new.

f. .... It looks like a bike you can ride on very rough mountains and over rocks.

11 **Put the sentences above in a logical order. Then write the sentences into a paragraph on a separate sheet of paper. Give the paragraph a title.**

Writing focus: Writing the paragraph

After you have chosen a topic and brainstormed ideas, it is time to write your paragraph.

- Choose a topic sentence first.
- Then write the supporting sentences.
- Finish with a concluding sentence.
- Give your paragraph a title.

But this is only the beginning! Good writers follow three steps to improve their writing. They ...

1. check their work.
2. show their work to someone else.
3. make any necessary additions and changes.

These steps can be repeated several times.

12 With a partner, describe the diagram below. What is happening in each circle?

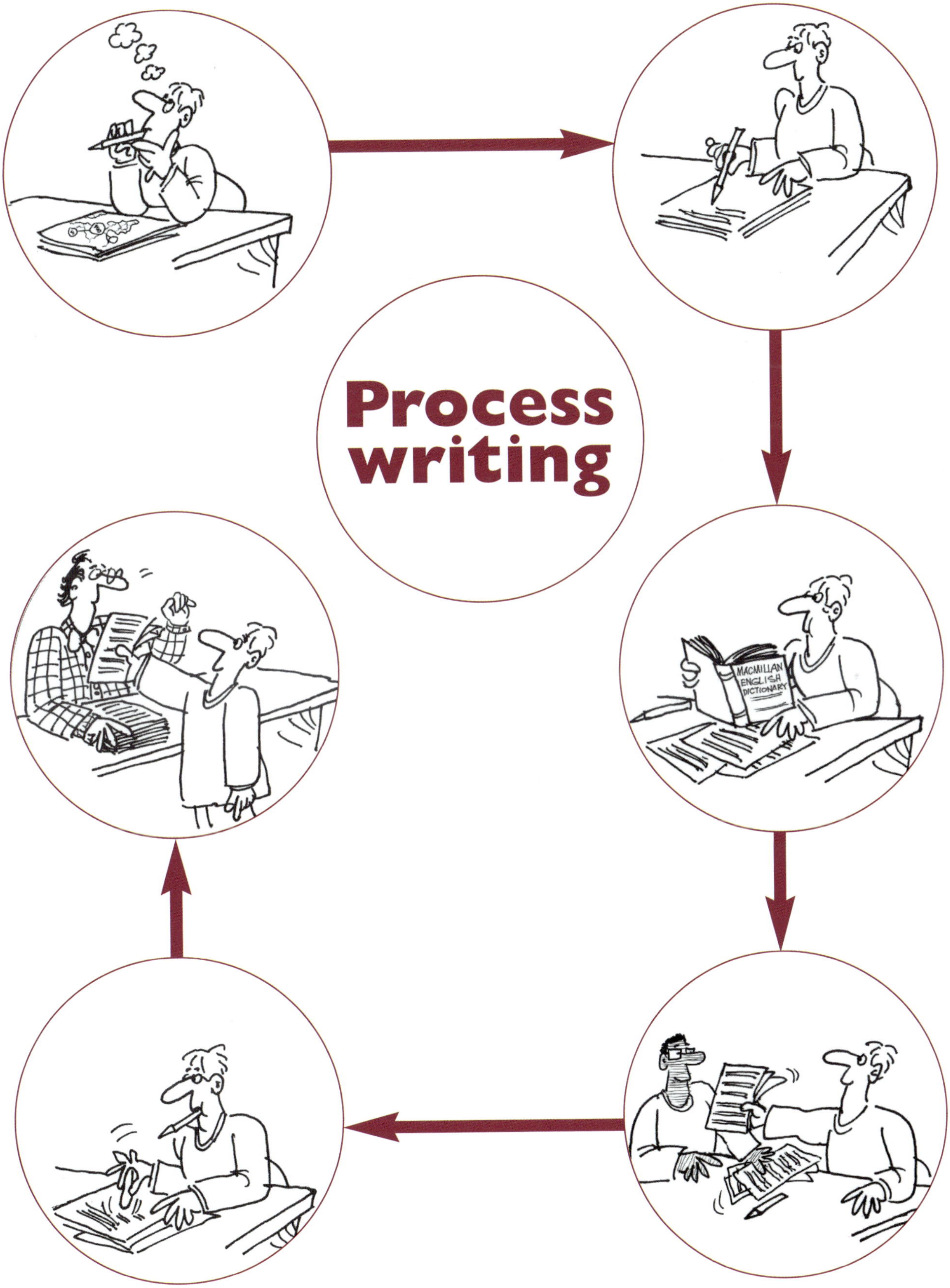

Writing focus: Peer reviewing

Exchanging papers with a classmate, reading each other's paper, and making comments is called *peer reviewing*. When you read a classmate's paper, you can ...

- practise finding topic sentences, supporting sentences, and concluding sentences.
- notice special vocabulary or grammar.
- see different ways to do the same assignment.
- help the writer by saying what ideas you liked best.
- ask questions to help the writer think of more ideas.
- ask a question if you don't understand something – and maybe the writer will think of a better way to explain.

Many writers – even very good writers – feel nervous or shy about sharing their writing. When you write comments about someone's writing, be kind, useful and truthful. Remember always to say what you like. Comment on ideas and organisation, and not spelling or grammar.

13 With a partner or group, look at the comments below. Put a tick (✓) by the ones that are useful for the writer. Put a cross (✗) by the ones that you think aren't useful and give a reason; for example:

- It isn't kind.
- It isn't clear.
- It isn't useful.
- It (probably) isn't true.

a. ☐ The topic sentence was really interesting.

b. ☐ You don't have any examples.

c. ☐ You have one good example. But your paragraph is a little short. Can you write another example?

d. ☐ I liked your paragraph because it was honest. I think you should add a title.

e. ☐ Your topic sentence and concluding sentence are exactly the same. Maybe one should be different.

f. ☐ I think it's OK.

g. ☐ Your paragraph is not very good. I couldn't understand anything.

h. ☐ Your concluding sentence was funny. I liked it a lot!

i. ☐ You used some interesting vocabulary. It was easy for me to imagine that place.

j. ☐ You are a better writer than Shakespeare!

k. ☐ I'm not sure which sentence is the topic sentence. Is it the first one or the second one? Please tell me.

Put it together

14 **Use the ideas from your brainstorming from exercises 5 and 8 on pages 36 and 37 to write a paragraph. Write a topic sentence and supporting sentences. Decide if you want to write a concluding sentence.**

15 **Check your writing.**

Did you ...

- ☐ include a heading on your paper?
- ☐ format the paragraph properly?
- ☐ start and end each sentence correctly?
- ☐ use capitalisation correctly?
- ☐ give the paragraph a title?
- ☐ write a topic sentence?
- ☐ write supporting sentences? How many?
- ☐ use descriptive adjectives?
- ☐ only include one clear idea in each sentence?
- ☐ order the sentences logically?
- ☐ combine sentences logically?
- ☐ write a concluding sentence?

16 **Exchange papers with a partner. Include your brainstorming.**

- Fill out the Peer Review Form on page 104.
- Talk with your partner and go over each form.

17 **Read your paragraph again.**

- Think about the comments from your partner.
- Make any additions or changes to your paragraph that would make it stronger or more interesting.

18 **Hand in the second draft of your paragraph to your teacher.**

6 White Lies

In this unit, you will ...

- **identify opinions and examples in supporting sentences.**
- **use discussion to brainstorm.**
- **write a paragraph about your opinions.**

1 **What is a *white lie*?**

a. A mistake about colours, e.g. 'Tom's new car is red' when it is actually purple.
b. A small or unimportant lie you tell not to hurt someone's feelings, e.g. 'I think your new car looks cool' when you actually think the new car looks ugly.
c. A type of lie politicians tell to be popular, e.g. 'When I am President, everyone will be able to buy a new car' when the politician knows people will not have more money.

- Tell a partner about the last time you told a white lie to a friend, a family member or a teacher.
- Tell your partner if you think it is OK to tell white lies.

2 **Now read this paragraph to find out if the writer agrees with you about telling white lies.**

White Lies

1. White lies are not always bad. 2. If you tell your girlfriend that her new haircut looks great when it is horrible, she will know you are lying. 3. I think it is better to tell the truth in this case. 4. However, if your girlfriend has a new dress and she really likes it, you should always say it is lovely. 5. If you say you don't like it, you will make her unhappy and angry with you. 6. You can lie if the truth will hurt and it is not important.

3 Read the paragraph on page 42, *White Lies*, again and answer these questions.

a. Which sentence is the topic sentence?

b. What does the concluding sentence do?
   1. It restates the topic sentence.
   2. It makes a prediction.
   3. It makes a suggestion.

c. What do sentences 2 and 4 do?
   1. They give advice.
   2. They give examples.
   3. They tell a story.

Language focus: Giving an opinion

Your *opinion* is your personal feeling. A *fact* is something that is true. Most writing uses both facts and opinions. When you talk about your opinions, you can start your sentence with phrases such as:

I think *friends should always be honest.*
I don't think *white lies are dangerous.*
I believe *it is better to upset your friends than to lie.*
In my view, *it is often safer to lie than to tell the truth.*
In my opinion, *lying is the same as cheating or stealing.*

When you write, you can use one of the sentence starters above. However, be careful not to use too many, or to use them too often. That can make your writing sound weak. The reader knows that the paragraph is your opinion, because you wrote it!

4 Look at the sentences below. Write F for the facts, and O for the opinions.

a. ...*O*... Learning English is easier for girls than for boys.
   ...*F*... There are more boys than girls in my English class.

b. .... Good teachers don't give too much homework.
   .... Our teacher gave us homework last week.

c. .... Keanu Reeves is a good actor.
   .... Keanu Reeves starred in the *Matrix* films.

d. .... Many teenagers carry mobile phones these days.
   .... Mobile phones are very convenient.

e. .... All students have to wear a uniform at my school.
   .... Our school uniforms are not very comfortable.

f. .... I don't believe that wearing the latest fashions is important.
   .... My favourite clothes are all black.

5 For each topic below, write one fact and one opinion.

- Read your sentences to a partner.
- Your partner will tell you which sentence is the fact and which is the opinion.

a. tea

Green tea is good for your health. *F* ....

Black tea tastes better than green tea. *O* ....

b. university entrance exams

....

....

c. violent video games

....

....

d. dating

....

....

e. money

....

....

f. sports

....

....

g. (your choice of topic)

....

....

Brainstorming: Discussion

Talking with other people is a good way to brainstorm:

- You can share ideas with different people.
- You can ask questions to help other students think more deeply.
- When other students ask you questions, you will think of examples to support your opinions.

When you're discussing, it's OK to disagree with your classmates. However, it is important to be respectful of opinions that are different from yours.

6 **In a group, form opinions about the topics below.**

- Think of as many opinions as you can. You don't have to believe them.
- Someone in your group should write down all the opinions in your group.
- Share your opinions with another group or with the whole class.

a. International marriages
b. Parents leaving a five-year-old child alone in the house
c. Secondary school students playing video games

Writing focus: Supporting sentences with opinions and examples

In your topic sentence and supporting sentences, you can give an opinion. To support your opinion, you could give *examples*, which can either be facts or experiences you've had.

7 **Look again at the paragraph on page 42, *White Lies*. Which sentences are opinions? Which sentences are examples? Are some sentences both?**

8 **Decide if these sentences are opinions (O) or examples (E). Write O or E next to each sentence.**

a. .... Smoking should be banned in all restaurants.

b. .... Smoking is banned in restaurants in California and New York.

c. .... The air is cleaner and healthier in non-smoking restaurants.

d. .... I believe that customers prefer non-smoking restaurants.

e. .... My clothes smelt horrible after I had dinner with a friend who smoked.

f. .... I went to a smoky restaurant in Paris, and I couldn't eat my food.

g. .... In my country, smoking is banned on buses and trains, and in all public buildings.

9 **Read this paragraph and answer the questions below.**

Lying

1. In my opinion, exaggeration is the same as lying. 2. My friend John is always exaggerating. 3. When we met two years ago, he told me he spoke French fluently. 4. However, last week we met a French man at a football match. 5. John couldn't say anything to him in French except, 'Where are you from?' and 'Do you like England?' 6. I think he lies because he wants to be exciting. 7. Last night, he told me he has a new millionaire girlfriend. 8. She probably has a lot of money but isn't a millionaire. 9. I don't believe John is a good friend.

a. Tick (✓) the writer's opinions.

1. ☐ A good friend doesn't exaggerate.

2. ☐ A good friend has a rich girlfriend.

3. ☐ A good friend is exciting.

4. ☐ A good friend tells the truth.

b. Underline two examples used to support the writer's opinions.

c. Work with a partner.

1. Give an example of a time you have told a white lie or exaggerated.

2. Tell your partner your opinion about white lies and exaggeration.

Put it together

10 Choose one of the opinions you wrote for exercise 6 on page 45.

- Use this opinion for your topic sentence.
- Brainstorm ideas by discussing the opinion with a small group.
- Write down examples (facts or experiences) to support your opinion.

11 Write a paragraph. Use opinions and examples.

12 Check your writing.

Did you ...

- ☐ include a heading on your paper?
- ☐ format the paragraph properly?
- ☐ start and end each sentence correctly?
- ☐ use capitalisation correctly?
- ☐ give the paragraph a title?
- ☐ write a topic sentence?
- ☐ write supporting sentences? How many?
- ☐ only include one clear idea in each sentence?
- ☐ order the sentences logically?
- ☐ combine the sentences logically?
- ☐ write a concluding sentence?

13 Exchange papers with a partner.

- Fill out the Peer Review Form on page 105.
- Talk with your partner and go over each form.

14 Read your paragraph again.

- Think about the comments from your partner.
- Make any additions or changes to your paragraph that would make it stronger or more interesting.

15 Hand in the second draft of your paragraph to your teacher.

7 Explanations and Excuses

In this unit, you will ...

- develop paragraphs which explain cause and effect / result.
- combine sentences with *so* and *because.*
- practise further with word maps and freewriting.
- write a paragraph about explanations and excuses.

1 **Describe this picture to a partner. Guess what the problem is. Tell your partner what you think the people are saying.**

2 **Read the paragraph and check your guess.**

It Wasn't My Fault!

1. Teachers should be understanding when students can't complete assignments on time. 2. I couldn't do the writing homework for English class today, and my teacher didn't want to hear my reasons. 3. I had good reasons, too. 4. Last night was Evan's birthday. 5. He's my best friend, so I had to go to his party. 6. After the party, I tried to do the homework, but my computer froze and I lost all the information. 7. I was too tired to write it again because it was very late. 8. My teacher didn't care. 9. She said, 'You had two weeks to do the assignment, so there are no excuses.' 10. I think she's angry with me, but it wasn't my fault.

3 Why didn't the writer do his homework? Write W for the writer's reasons and T for the teacher's reasons.

The writer didn't do his homework because ...

a .... it was his best friend's birthday.

b. .... he is lazy.

c. .... he isn't organised.

d. .... he had a computer problem.

e. .... he isn't a serious student.

Language focus: Giving explanations

Cause and effect / result

- *So* and *because* can be used to join two sentences together:

It was raining. I took an umbrella.
It was raining, **so** *I took an umbrella.*
I took an umbrella **because** *it was raining.*

- *So* and *because* have a similar function.

So tells us the result or effect of a situation:
I took an umbrella.

Because tells us why something happens (the cause):
I took an umbrella. Why? Because it was raining.

- *So* and *because* are often very close in meaning, and you can choose either – but you must use *so* with the result / effect and *because* with the cause:

I had a cold. I didn't go to class.
I had a cold, **so** *I didn't go to class.*
I didn't go to class **because** *I had a cold.*

Note: A comma comes before *so*. There is no comma before *because*.

4 Look again at the paragraph on page 48, *It Wasn't My Fault*, and do the following.

a. Underline the sentences that use *so* or *because*.
b. For each of those sentences, tell a partner what part of the sentence tells the *cause* and what part tells the *effect / result*.

5 **Write a sentence using *so* and another sentence using *because* for these situations.**

a. The film was boring. I left early.

*The film was boring, **so** I left early.* ....

*I left early **because** the film was boring.* ....

b. We played badly. We lost the football match.

....

....

c. I failed the test. I didn't study hard.

....

....

d. My alarm clock didn't work. I was late for the meeting.

....

....

e. I am shy. I don't have a girlfriend.

....

....

f. I won't go to the party. I'm tired.

....

....

Language focus: Starting with because

Look at these two sentences:

I was too tired to write it again **because** *it was very late.*
Because *it was very late, I was too tired to write it again.*

There is no difference in meaning between these two sentences. When you write, use both styles. This will make your writing more varied and more interesting. However, there is a difference in punctuation.

6 **With a partner, find the difference in punctuation. Write the explanation here.**

....

....

....

7 **Rewrite these sentences using *because*.**

a. I couldn't bring my homework. My dog ate my homework.

I couldn't bring my homework ***because*** *my dog ate it.*

Because *my dog ate my homework, I couldn't bring it.*

b. I am too busy. I don't exercise.

....

....

c. I have too much homework. I go to bed late.

....

....

d. I can't give up smoking. I will put on weight.

....

....

e. I lost my friend's book. I was careless.

....

....

f. I'm not going to go to the beach. I have to take an exam.

....

....

Brainstorming: Practice with word maps and freewriting

8 **Look at this word map and answer the questions below.**

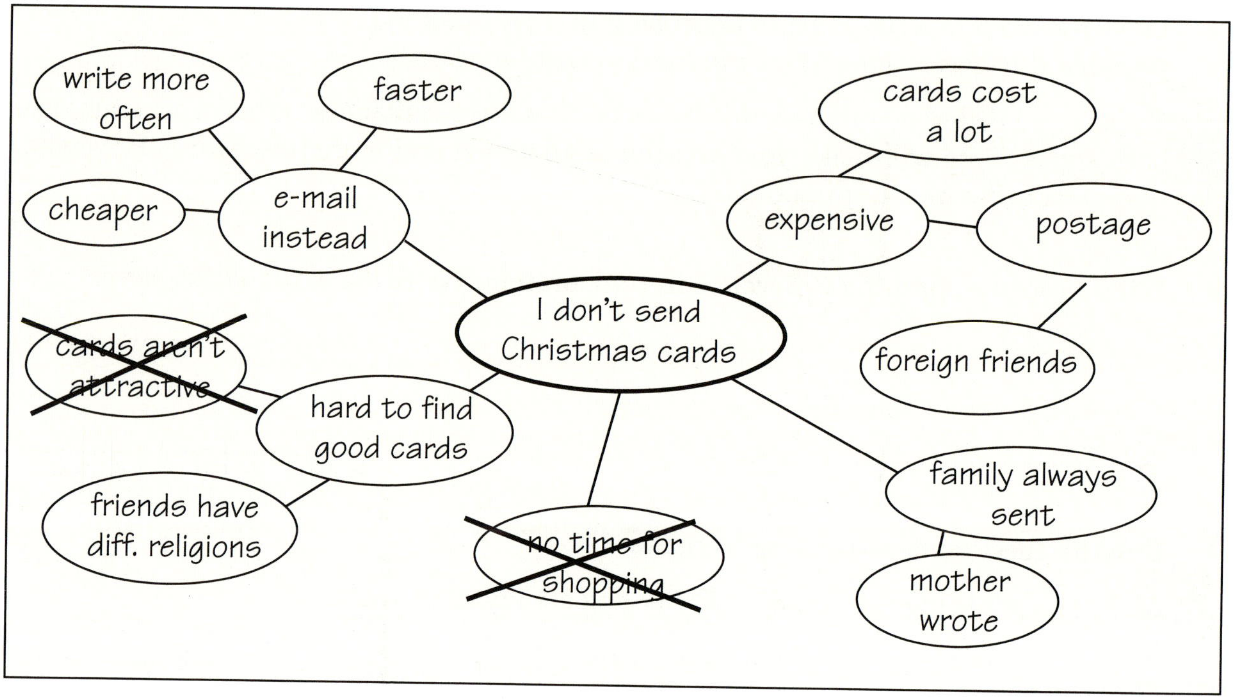

a. What is the writer's topic?
b. How many examples does the writer have?
c. Why did the writer cross out some ideas?

9 **Read this paragraph. Were your guesses from exercise 8 above correct? Look at the word map again, and write a topic sentence for the paragraph. Then complete the paragraph with *so* or *because*.**

Why I Don't Send Christmas Cards

My family has always sent Christmas cards to friends. ....
....
One reason is that I have friends all over the world, [a] .... sending cards to them would be expensive. In addition, it's difficult to choose the right cards [b] .... my friends have different religious beliefs.

Finally, I e-mail my friends almost every week. [c] .... I contact them so often, I don't have anything special to say at holiday times. Even though I don't send Christmas cards, I am still close to my friends.

10 **Look at this picture, and think about what is happening.**

11 **Freewrite for five minutes about how the driver explains the cause of the accident.**

> **Remember**
> When you are freewriting, ...
> - write for five minutes without stopping.
> - write as much as you can. You can cross out ideas you don't like later.
> - don't worry about spelling, grammar, or organisation.

12 **Check and edit your freewriting. Using your ideas, write at least three sentences with *so* or *because*. Then share your sentences with a partner or small group.**

Put it together

13 **Choose one of these topics and make a word map or freewrite to get some ideas.**

a. A time I was late
b. An accident
c. A mistake
d. It wasn't my fault!

14 **Edit your brainstorming. Cross out ideas you don't want to use and add more ideas if necessary.**

15 **Write a paragraph about your topic and then check your writing.**

16 **Exchange papers with a partner. Include your brainstorming.**

- Fill out the Peer Review Form on page 106.
- Talk with your partner and go over each form.

17 **Read your paragraph again.**

- Think about the comments from your partner.
- Make any additions or changes to your paragraph that would make it stronger or more interesting.

18 **Hand in the second draft of your paragraph to your teacher.**

8 *Problems*

In this unit, you will ...

- **express personal feelings about problems.**
- **practise using *would like to*, *want to* and *have to*.**
- **learn to order supporting sentences logically.**
- **edit lists by ordering ideas logically.**
- **write about problems or difficulties.**

1 In a small group, describe problems you have with one of the following:

- family and friends
- teachers, classes and studying
- money and budgeting
- expressing your feelings and ideas

2 This paragraph is about a problem with parents. Read the paragraph to see if you share the problem and if you agree with the writer.

Talking to Parents

1. Talking to friends and classmates is easy for a lot of teenage boys, but talking to parents is more difficult. 2. Many teenage boys would like to talk to their fathers about their feelings, but they don't know how. 3. Sons often want to know how their fathers feel about them. 4. For example, I would like my father to say that he is proud of me. 5. However, my father never talks about his feelings. 6. He only wants to talk about sports or my schoolwork. 7. Parents have to talk to their kids about their feelings, or their children will feel lonely at home.

3 **With a partner, answer these questions.**

a. Which sentence is the topic sentence?
b. What does the concluding sentence do? (You can tick more than one answer.)

1. ☐ It restates the topic sentence.
2. ☐ It makes a prediction.
3. ☐ It makes a suggestion.
4. ☐ It summarises the paragraph.

c. Which of these details and examples could be added to the paragraph on page 55? Explain why the others do not belong.

1. ☐ My father is 58 years old.
2. ☐ My father's parents don't talk about their feelings either.
3. ☐ My father is often busy with his job, so I don't have many chances to see him.
4. ☐ Many parents like to play tennis and golf at the weekend.
5. ☐ It's also hard to choose a good birthday present for my father.
6. ☐ I guess if I want to talk with my father, I will have to start more conversations myself.

Language focus: Want to, would like to, have to

Want to and *would like to* are useful expressions for talking about wishes:
I **want to** *get a good job.*
Miwa **would like to** *travel overseas.*

Note: In speech and informal writing, the contraction *I'd like to* is often used. However, in academic writing, contractions are less common. Use *I would like to* when you write.

Have to shows *obligation* (that you must do something, or that it is required):
Mei Mei **has to** *get up early to get to school on time.*
If you want to drive a car, you **have to** *get a driver's licence.*

4 **Read the paragraph on page 55, *Talking to Parents*, again and underline the sentences containing *want to*, *would like to* and *have to*.**

5 **Complete these sentences with the correct form of *want to*, *would like to*, or *have to*.**

a. Kelly .... clean her room. It's a mess!

b. Ji Eun .... take dance lessons, but she doesn't have enough money.

c. Evan and Erik .... go to the party, but no-one can give them a lift.

d. I .... go out last night, but I .... work at my part-time job.

e. My parents say if I want a new bicycle, I will .... pay for it myself.

f. If you .... work in Spain, you .... learn Spanish.

g. My little sister is always bothering me when I .... be alone.

6 **Complete these sentences. Then share with a partner.**

a. I would like ....

b. I have to ....

c. I want to .... , but I have to ....

d. When I was a child, I wanted to ....

e. Last year, I had to ....

f. I wish I didn't have to .... !

8

Writing focus: Order of supporting ideas

After brainstorming ideas for a paragraph, you need to decide which ideas to use and the order you will write the ideas.

Ideas and sentences need to be ordered logically.

- Sentences that are part of the same idea go together.
- Sentences can go in *chronological* (time) order.
- Sentences can go in order of importance (see explanation below).

One way to organise your supporting sentences is to decide which ideas are most important. Writers often put the most important ideas last in a paragraph, so the strongest sentences are the last ones the reader sees. When you edit ideas in a list, you can number them in order of importance.

Remember
When brainstorming, ...
- use a separate, whole sheet of paper.
- collect as many ideas as possible (don't stop writing).
- don't worry if you don't like the ideas.
- write short phrases or single words for lists and word maps, and sentences for freewriting.
- after you brainstorm, look at the relevant ideas and brainstorm again.
- edit your brainstorming before you write your paragraph.

7 **Look at the list of ideas for a paragraph called *Making Language Classes Interesting*.**

- Number the brainstormed ideas in order of importance (write 1 by the most important idea, 2 by the second most important idea, and so on).
- The writer decided not to use two details from the list. Which were they, and why?

...... studied for 7 years, can't speak (topic sentence?)
...... got better grades in Spanish
...... French textbooks old
   old photos
   no popular culture
   famous people were dead!
...... class has to be interesting!
   music / films / games
...... learn about culture, talk about life
...... boring French classes
   too much memorisation and grammar
...... best friend (Linda) was in the same class

8 **Read the paragraph *Making Language Classes Interesting* to see if the writer's order of importance was the same as yours.**

Making Language Classes Interesting

1. Learning a language is difficult, but it doesn't have to be boring. 2. I studied French at school for seven years, but I cannot speak a word of French now. 3. The problem with learning French was my classes, not the language. 4. One problem was that our textbooks were too old and boring. 5. The pictures were black and white, and the famous singers and film stars had already died! 6. We also wanted to learn about popular French culture and talk about our lives in French. 7. Students do not want to memorise rules and vocabulary for an hour everyday and nothing else. 8. The most important point is that the classroom has to be interesting. 9. Students need to play games, listen to music, watch films and talk about them in the foreign language. 10. Teachers need to make language classes useful and interesting if they want students to learn.

9 **Look at these sentences for a paragraph called *The Challenge of Running a Marathon*. Number the sentences in chronological order.**

- [1] Last year I ran the London marathon, and it was the hardest thing I've ever done.
- [ ] The twenty-mile point was the worst because I had been running for three hours, I was hungry, and I was in a lot of pain.
- [ ] The beginning of the race was a lot of fun because the crowd was cheering and the sun was shining.
- [ ] I had to spend about six months training for the marathon before it even started.
- [ ] When I crossed the finish line, I could hardly walk and I felt sick.
- [ ] Next year, I would like to watch the marathon but not run it.
- [ ] After thirteen miles, the middle of the marathon, my legs began to hurt and I started to get bored.
- [ ] On the day of the marathon, I had to get up at 5 a.m. and get to the starting line. It was cold, and everyone was very tired.

10 **Look at the paragraph *Not Enough Time* below and do the following.**

a. Choose *three* of the supporting ideas below the paragraph.
b. Write the sentences into the paragraph.
c. Put the most important example last.
d. Share your paragraph with a partner.

> **Note:** It's OK to have a different order – but be sure to explain your choices!

Not Enough Time

Should I quit my part-time job? I like my job as a waiter in a Chinese restaurant because the food is good, the atmosphere is friendly, and I can earn some money. But it is causing some problems for me.

Even though I like my job, I might quit until I finish school, or ask my boss if I can work fewer hours.

- The cooks let me test the food sometimes, and I am gaining weight.
- I would like to see my friends more often, but I have to work almost every night.
- It's hard for me to finish my homework. I want to concentrate on my studies, but I am too tired after work.
- I want to be a journalist and I would like to spend my free time writing stories about the people in my town. I can't do this and work so many hours.
- I have to drive to work, and my car is very old. I'm afraid it will wear out because I am driving it too much.

11 **Look again at the paragraph on page 60, *Not Enough Time*. Why did the writer begin with a question? Share your ideas with a partner or group.**

a. The writer didn't know some information.
b. The writer wanted to get some advice from another person.
c. To make the reader interested in the topic.
d. The writer didn't understand the topic very well.

Put it together

12 **Choose one of these topics and then brainstorm the topic by making a list.**

a. A problem with a friend
b. A problem at school
c. A problem at work
d. A problem in your city / school

13 **Edit your list.**

- Cross out ideas you don't want to use and add more ideas if necessary.
- Number the other ideas in order of importance.
- Share your list with a partner, and explain your choices.

14 **Write a paragraph about your topic and then check your writing.**

15 **Exchange papers with a partner. Include your brainstorming.**

- Fill out the Peer Review Form on page 107.
- Talk with your partner and go over each form.

16 **Read your paragraph again.**

- Think about the comments from your partner.
- Make any additions or changes to your paragraph that would make it stronger or more interesting.

17 **Hand in the second draft of your paragraph to your teacher.**

9 Strange Stories

In this unit you will ...

- **use time expressions: *after*, *before* and *when*.**
- **learn to identify the main parts of a narrative.**
- **practise ordering the events in a narrative in a logical way.**
- **write a paragraph about interesting or unusual experiences.**

1 Look at the picture. What do you think is happening? Share your ideas with a partner or group. Then read the paragraph below and check your guesses.

A UFO Sighting

1. I never believed in aliens before one night last year. 2. It was a cold, dark winter evening, and I was walking home from a friend's house. 3. I stopped to tie my shoe. 4. When I looked up again, I saw a round object coming towards me. 5. It was very large and shiny. 6. I couldn't believe what I was seeing. 7. Before I could shout or run, the object suddenly moved and then disappeared. 8. After the object disappeared, I ran all the way home and called my best friend. 9. When she picked up the phone, I couldn't say anything. 10. I knew she would think I was crazy. 11. I never told anyone about my UFO sighting.

2 Read the paragraph in exercise 1 above again and answer these questions.

a. Which sentence is the topic sentence?

b. How is this paragraph developed?
   1. by telling a story
   2. by giving reasons
   3. by describing objects with details

c. What does sentence 2 do?
   1. It gives details about the topic sentence.
   2. It tells the reader when and where the event happened.
   3. It lets the reader know the paragraph will talk about UFOs.

d. Is sentence 11 a concluding sentence?

Language focus: Using time expressions

One way to order two events is to use *after, before,* or *when.*

After shows the first event:
I played football **after school**. (school happened first; not football)
After school, *I played football.*

Before shows the second event:
I couldn't play the guitar **before I took lessons**. (lessons happened second)
Before I took lessons, *I couldn't play the guitar.*

When shows that the first event happened just before the second event:
I told him the news **when he called**. (he called first; then I told him the news)
When he called, *I told him the news.*

Note: When *after, before,* or *when* begin a sentence, use a comma after the event.

3 Join these ideas with *after, before,* or *when*. Add a comma if necessary.

a. After the film, we went home.

d. I left my house .... you called.

b. We left the class .... we handed in our assignments.

e Please finish your homework .... you watch TV!

c. I woke up .... the alarm clock rang.

f. .... the dog barked, the baby cried.

4 **Look at these pictures. What strange thing happened? Share your guesses with a partner.**

5 **Read the paragraph *Sleeping in a Farmhouse* to see if your guess in exercise 4 above was correct. Then complete the paragraph with *after*, *before*, or *when*.**

Sleeping in a Farmhouse

The strangest experience in my life happened a year [a] .... I finished school. I was sixteen years old and my best friend Mark was fifteen. He invited me to visit him during the summer. I was staying with him in his farmhouse in the middle of the countryside. I shared a room with Mark, and our beds were separated by a table. Every morning, Mark's mum brought us a cup of hot tea in bed [b] .... we woke up. While we were sleeping one night, I could feel my bed moving. I thought I was dreaming. The next morning, Mark's mother brought us hot tea as usual. [c] .... she turned on the lights, we saw that our beds were pushed together and the table had moved. Mark said he didn't do it, and I didn't do it. We still don't know how the beds moved! What do you think?

6 **With a partner, think of different explanations for why the beds moved. (You can draw a picture of what happened to help explain.) Then share your ideas with another pair or the whole class.**

Writing focus: Narrative paragraphs

Narratives tell stories. Everyone has read narratives, watched them on television or at the cinema, or heard them from other people. A narrative paragraph tells a short story or describes an event.

The paragraph *Sleeping in a Farmhouse* is a narrative about two boys on holiday. In the story their beds move in the middle of the night, and they don't know how it happened.

The events (stages of the story) are told in a logical order:

1. **Background information**

   A narrative paragraph usually starts with background information to set the scene for the story and provide context. It can tell **when** and **where** a story happened:

   > The strangest experience in my life happened a year before I finished school. I was sixteen years old and my best friend Mark was fifteen. He invited me to visit him during the summer.

2. **Beginning of the story**

   The beginning of a narrative usually tells what happened first in the story:

   > I was staying with him in his farmhouse in the middle of the countryside. I shared a room with Mark, and our beds were separated by a table. Every morning, Mark's mum brought us a cup of hot tea in bed after we woke up.

3. **Middle of the story**

   The middle of the narrative is usually the main part and tells most of the events in the story:

   > While we were sleeping one night, I could feel my bed moving. I thought I was dreaming. The next morning, Mark's mother brought us hot tea as usual. When she turned on the lights, we saw that our beds were pushed together and the table had moved.

4. **End of the story**

   The end of a narrative concludes the story. It tells the final event, and has a concluding remark:

   > Mark said he didn't do it, and I didn't do it. We still don't know how the beds moved! What do you think?

7 **Look at these pictures from a story. In a small group, describe what happened.**

a

b

c

8 **Read these parts of a paragraph about the pictures in exercise 7 above. Decide if the parts are ...**

- background information.
- from the beginning of the story.
- from the middle of the story.
- from the end of the story.

Then number the parts in the correct order. (There are two parts of the middle section.)

a. ☐ ....

A few days later my father was able to go to the window to look for himself. But all he could see was an ugly brick wall.

b. ☐ ....

A strange thing happened to my father when he was in hospital to have an operation.

c. ☐ ....

The next day he asked the nurse why the man described a beautiful park. The nurse looked confused and told my father, 'That man was blind'.

d. ☐ ....

My father didn't feel well. He asked the other man to describe the view outside the window because he wanted to feel better. After the man talked about the beautiful view from the window, my father was able to fall asleep. Before my father woke up, the man left the hospital.

e. ☐ ....

After his operation, my father woke up sharing a room with another man. The other man's bed was next to the window.

9 **Read the parts below of two stories, *A Fright in the Forest* and *A Strange Day in Class*. Number the parts in the correct order and decide if they are ...**

- background information.
- from the beginning of the story.
- from the middle of the story.
- from the end of the story.

Note: The middle parts are not complete!

A Fright in the Forest

a. ☐ ....
Suddenly, I felt very cold and scared.

b. ☐ ....
I grew up in a small village in the countryside. Near my house was a large forest, and my parents told me not to play there.

c. ☐ ....
After that day, I never went back to the forest.

d. ☐ ....
One day, I was playing in the forest with some of my school friends.

A Strange Day in Class

a. ☐ ....
I have been studying English for a few years and I really enjoy the classes.

b. ☐ ....
I heard everyone laughing. I woke up and realised it was a dream.

c. ☐ ....
One day something unusual happened in class.

d. ☐ ....
The teacher was explaining grammar when I saw something strange out of the window.

10 **With a partner, brainstorm what happened in each story. Then write sentences to complete the middle part of each story. Share your paragraph with another pair or the class.**

Remember
Brainstorming ...
- helps you collect ideas.
- helps you be creative and imaginative.
- can be done by discussing ideas.

Put it together

11 **Choose one of these topics.**

a. A coincidence
b. A strange experience
c. A funny story

12 **Choose one of the methods of brainstorming you have practised, and brainstorm the story.**

- making a list
- making a word map
- freewriting
- discussion

13 **Edit your brainstorming.**

- Cross out ideas you don't want to use and add more ideas if necessary.
- Share your brainstorming with a partner, and explain your choices.

14 **Write a paragraph about your topic and then check your writing.**

15 **Exchange papers with a partner. Include your brainstorming.**

- Fill out the Peer Review Form on page 108.
- Talk with your partner and go over each form.

16 **Work with a new partner. Tell him / her about the story that you read in exercise 15 above. Listen to your partner tell someone else's story.**

17 **Read your paragraph again.**

- Think about the comments from your partner.
- Make any additions or changes to your paragraph that would make it stronger or more interesting.

18 **Hand in the second draft of your paragraph to your teacher.**

10 *Differences*

In this unit, you will ...

- use double lists to brainstorm.
- use *whereas* and *however* to make comparisons.
- learn to organise a comparison paragraph.
- compare different situations / events.
- write a paragraph about the changes in your life.

1 **Look at the pictures. Tell a partner what you think the differences are between secondary school and university life for this woman.**

2 **Read this paragraph and find out the important differences for the writer.**

University Life

1. My life changed a lot when I was at university. 2. There were 600 students at my school and I knew nearly everyone. 3. However, there were thousands of students at my university, and I didn't know anyone. 4. I felt very lonely. 5. At school, the classes were half boys and half girls. 6. At university, I studied engineering, and there weren't many women in the classes. 7. The biggest change at university was the style of class. 8. We had to do a lot of reading and learning on our own, whereas at school the teacher told us nearly everything to study for the exams. 9. Even though university was more difficult, I enjoyed it more than my school days – after I got used to it!

3 **Read the paragraph on page 69, *University Life*, again and answer these questions with a partner.**

a. How many differences between secondary school and university does the writer mention? What are they?

b. The writer says that the biggest difference between school and university was the style of class. Do you think this was a positive or negative difference? Explain your opinion to a partner.

c. What are or what will be the differences for you between school and university?

Brainstorming: Double lists

4 **Look at the pictures and tell a partner how you think the summer and winter are different in the Pyrenees.**

5 **Read this paragraph and decide if the writer prefers the summer or winter in the Pyrenees.**

Winter in the Pyrenees

[1] Spend a year in the Pyrenees and you'll be amazed by the difference between the summer and winter seasons. [2] The summer season is warm, and everyone likes to go walking and climbing. [3] People also go on hikes in the many mountains and watch the wildlife. [4] Summer in the Pyrenees is very green, and many tourists visit the countryside. [5] However, the winter is even more spectacular. [6] It snows a lot in the Pyrenees in the winter, and the scenery looks beautiful. [7] It is great for skiing and snowboarding as there are lots of different runs through forests and open areas. [8] You can even try your hand at tobogganing or dogsledding. [9] In the evenings, you can warm up in one of the tapas bars or French cafés, depending on which side of the border you are.

6 **Read the paragraph again and look at this brainstormed list. Underline the ideas the writer used from it.**

Summer		Winter	
warm	hiking in mountains	cold	tobogganing / dogsledding
climbing	air-conditioning	parties	snow boarding / skiing
shorts / T-Shirts	long, sunny days	scarves / hats / gloves	short, dark days
sunglasses	holiday	snow	French cafés
watching wildlife	my birthday	beautiful scenery	tapas bars

Note: The writer used a *double list* technique to brainstorm ideas for the paragraph describing differences between summer and winter in the Pyrenees. A double list is useful when you are comparing two subjects.

7 **Choose one of the topics below. Use a double list to brainstorm ideas.**

- Share your list with a partner.
- Discuss which ideas would be good to write about.

a. Primary school / secondary school
b. Last year's fashions / this year's fashions
c. My best friend five years ago / my best friend now
d. What was important to me at thirteen years old / what is important now

Language focus: However / whereas

However and *whereas* can be used to connect two different or opposite ideas:

my friends prefer watching films / I find books more interesting
My friends prefer watching films. **However,** *I find books more interesting.*
My friends prefer watching films, **whereas** *I find books more interesting.*
Whereas *my friends prefer watching films, I find books more interesting.*

Note: You can join two sentences with *whereas.* Use *whereas* at the beginning of a sentence or in the middle, after a comma. Use *however* at the beginning of a sentence.

8 **Look again at the paragraph on page 69, *University Life* and the paragraph on page 70, *Winter in the Pyrenees*. Underline the sentences that use *however* and *whereas*. Note the punctuation used with these words.**

9 **Connect these ideas with *whereas* or *however*. Add punctuation where needed.**

a. (*however*) skiing is a popular winter sport / many young people prefer snowboarding
b. (*whereas* first) my science class has over 300 people in it / my English seminar has just twelve
c. (*whereas* in the middle) dogs are more faithful / cats are more independent
d. (*however*) cars are faster / I'd rather ride my bicycle
e. (*however*) DVDs are more common these days / I have a huge video collection
f. (*whereas*) (your ideas)

Writing focus: Organising a comparison paragraph

When you compare two things (secondary school life and university life; summer and winter weather), you have two choices for organising your paragraph:

- You can write all about the first subject and then all about the second (*block style*).

First block about the summer in the Pyrenees.

Second block about the winter in the Pyrenees.

Winter in the Pyrenees

1. Spend a year in the Pyrenees and you'll be amazed by the difference between the summer and winter seasons. 2. The summer season is warm, and everyone likes to go walking and climbing. 3. People also go on hikes in the many mountains and watch the wildlife. 4. Summer in the Pyrenees is very green, and many tourists visit the countryside. 5. However, the winter is even more spectacular. 6. It snows a lot in the Pyrenees in the winter, and the scenery looks beautiful. 7. It is great for skiing and snowboarding as there are lots of different runs through forests and open areas. 8. You can even try your hand at tobogganing or dogsledding. 9. In the evenings, you can warm up in one of the tapas bars or French cafés, depending on which side of the border you are.

- You can choose several points of comparison. Compare first one point about the two topics, then compare a second point about the two topics, and so on (*point-by-point style*).

First point about class size.

Second point about the number of boys and girls.

Third point about the class style.

University Life

1. My life changed a lot when I was at university. 2. There were 600 students at my secondary school and I knew nearly everyone. 3. However, there were thousands of students at my university and I didn't know anyone. 4. I felt very lonely. 5. At school the classes were half boys and half girls. 6. At university I studied engineering and there weren't many women in the classes. 7. The biggest change at university was the style of class. 8. We had to do a lot of reading and learning on our own, whereas at school the teacher told us nearly everything to study for the exams. 9. Even though university was more difficult, I enjoyed my life more than my school days – after I got used to it!

10 Look at the maps of the UK and Australia.

a. In a small group, discuss what you think the differences are between London and Sydney in December.

b. Make notes of the differences.

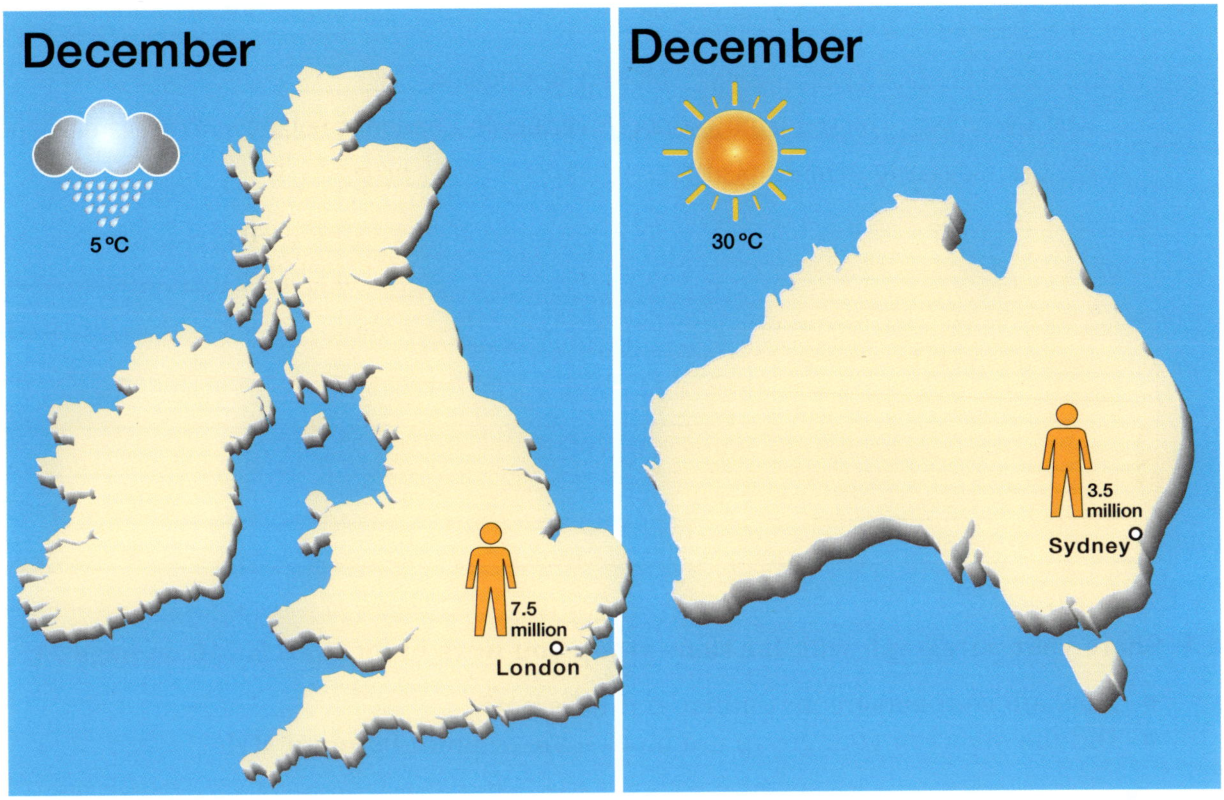

11 Look at the double list of characteristics of London and Sydney, and add your differences. With a partner, write sentences about the differences using *however* and *whereas*.

London	Sydney
in the northern hemisphere	in the southern hemisphere
difficult to make friends	easy to make friends
everyone stayed inside and watched TV	everyone was outside surfing and having barbeques

12 **On your own, complete the paragraph below, comparing London with Sydney.**

- Using exercises 10 and 11 on page 73, write supporting sentences for the paragraph.
- Remember to arrange the ideas in either block style or point-by-point style.
- Connect at least two ideas with *however* or *whereas*.
- Finish the paragraph with a concluding sentence.

Moving to England

Last December, I moved from Sydney, Australia to London, England with my family, and it was like moving to another planet.

13 **Share your paragraph with the same group you were in for exercise 10 on page 73.**

- How are your paragraphs similar and different?
- Did the others in your group use block style or point-by-point style?

Put it together

14 **Look at the brainstorming you did for exercise 7 on page 71.**

- Edit your brainstorming for a paragraph (or, if you wish, brainstorm again on one of the other topics).
- Decide if you will organise your paragraph in block style or point-by-point style.
- Number your ideas in order of importance.

15 **Write your paragraph and then check your writing.**

16 **Exchange papers with a partner. Include your brainstorming.**

- Fill out the Peer Review Form on page 109.
- Talk with your partner and go over each form.

17 **Read your paragraph again and make changes to improve it.**

18 **Hand in the second draft of your paragraph to your teacher.**

11 *Difficult Decisions*

In this unit, you will ...

- **practise writing about cause and effect relationships.**
- **use pair interviews to brainstorm.**
- **learn how to begin paragraphs with a question.**
- **write a paragraph about a difficult decision.**

1 Talk with a partner or small group. Is it important to keep secrets? Are there any secrets you would tell? Has anyone ever told a secret of yours? Why? How did you feel about it?

Telling a Secret

1. Do you think it's OK to tell your best friend's secret? 2. Last year, my best friend told me a secret, and she made me promise not to tell anyone. 3. My friend is slim, but she thought she was fat. 4. Consequently, she wouldn't eat any food, and she became anorexic. 5. I didn't know what to do. 6. Because I thought she might get angry, I hesitated to tell her parents or teachers. 7. However, I finally decided to tell her parents. 8. As a result, they made sure my friend ate all her meals. 9. They also took her to a psychologist every week for six months. 10. Because of her parents' and the psychologist's help, my friend is much healthier now. 11. I thought my friend would hate me for telling her parents about her problem, but last week she thanked me. 12. I'm glad I told her secret.

2 Read the paragraph above and discuss with a partner. Which of these events happened first? Write 1 by the first one and 2 by the second.

a. .... My friend thought she was fat. .... My friend wouldn't eat any food.
b. .... I hesitated to tell her parents. .... I thought she might get angry.
c. .... Her parents made sure she ate all her meals. .... I told her parents her secret.
d. .... My friend is healthier now. .... Her parents and the psychologist helped her.

3 Why did the writer start her paragraph with a question?

a. She wanted her readers' opinions about her decision.
b. She needed some information she didn't have.
c. She wanted her readers to think deeply about her topic.
d. She is worried she made the wrong decision.

4 How did the writer develop her paragraph?

a. She gave a lot of examples.
b. She used a narrative.
c. She described her friend carefully.

Language focus: Cause and effect

Remember
In Unit 7, you used *so* and *because* to write about cause and effect.
Because tells us the cause of an action or a situation.
So tells us the effect.

Below are some words and expressions, which, like *so*, show effect.
Use a variety of expressions in your writing to keep it interesting.

As a result, *consequently* and *therefore* are all used to connect two ideas. They all have a similar meaning. They show that the second sentence was the effect, or result, of the first one. They can be used at the beginning of the second sentence or they can join the two sentences with the word *and* before them.

as a result
I finally decided to tell her parents. **As a result,** *they made sure my friend ate all her meals.*
I finally decided to tell her parents, and **as a result** *they made sure my friend ate all her meals.*

consequently
My friend thought she was fat. **Consequently,** *she wouldn't eat any food.*
My friend thought she was fat, and **consequently** *she wouldn't eat any food.*

therefore
My friend thought she was fat. **Therefore,** *she wouldn't eat any food.*
My friend thought she was fat, and **therefore** *she wouldn't eat any food.*

5 Look at the example sentences above.

a. If *as a result*, *consequently*, or *therefore* begin a sentence, where is a comma used?
b. If they join two sentences with *and*, where is a comma used?

6 Connect these sentences with *as a result*, *consequently*, or *therefore*. Think about the correct order of the sentences and use correct punctuation.

a. I didn't go to university right away. I wanted to travel for a year after school.
b. My parents needed help in their restaurant. I moved back home and worked for them.
c. Cars are very convenient. People use them more than they should.
d. I told Tim that I couldn't go out with him. My parents didn't want me to date before I finished school.
e. Our school didn't have a lot of money. The administration decided to cancel some after-school clubs.
f. My friends complained that it was hard to communicate with me. I bought a mobile phone, even though I don't like them.

Brainstorming: Pair interviews

You have already used discussion for brainstorming in Unit 6. Talking with just one person can also help you think of ideas for writing because that person can ask you focused questions about your topic. Your partner might ask you questions that begin with words like *what, why, how long, when* and so on.

For example, when the writer of *Telling a Secret* told her partner about her difficult decision, her partner asked her questions such as *When did this happen? How did you find out about her problem? Why didn't you tell her parents immediately? What happened next? How did you feel? Do you think you made the right decision?*

To use pair interviews effectively, follow these steps:

- Tell your partner as much as you can about your topic.
- When you run out of things to say, your partner will ask you questions to help you continue.
- Write down the ideas that you talk about.

You won't use all of the ideas for your paragraph. However, it's always better to have too many ideas and then edit them.

7 With a partner, look at the pictures of a woman who had to make a difficult decision, and do the following.

a. Tell your partner what's happening in each picture.
b. Write a list of questions that you could ask the woman about her difficult decision.
c. Share your list of questions with another pair.

a b c

8 **Read this paragraph. Did the writer answer any of the questions you wrote with your partner?**

> *Studying Abroad*
>
> *1. Going to Australia was a difficult decision for me. 2. I wanted to go to Australia to get a degree in Business Administration, but my parents didn't want me to leave home. 3. I knew I would miss my friends and family too, because I would be in Australia for four years. 4. In the end, I decided to study in Australia to improve my career. 5. As a result, I now speak English very well, and I work for a large international company. 6. Because of all the languages I speak, I also travel around the world a lot with my company. 7. Therefore, I don't regret going to Australia.*

9 **Choose one of these topics. Then work with a partner. Your partner will ask you questions about your topic. Write down your partner's questions. At the end of the exercise, tell your partner which questions were the most helpful (helped you think of the most or the best ideas).**

a. Telling a secret / keeping a secret
b. A time I changed my mind
c. Choosing a job
d. Choosing a school / university
e. Starting / stopping an activity

Writing focus: Using questions to catch attention

A question at the beginning of your paragraph can encourage your reader to think deeply about your topic. Questions can be used to start paragraphs about a difficult decision, opinions, or personal feelings. In the opening paragraph in this unit, the writer asked, *Do you think it's OK to tell your best friend's secret?* This question helps the reader to think about the topic of secrets and telling them.

However, questions can be difficult to use effectively. The best questions are ones that help the reader to focus on and think about your topic. You need to imagine your audience (the people who will read your writing) and imagine how they might answer the question.

- Will the answer be too easy or too obvious?
- Could the reader give an answer very different from yours?

If the writer of *Telling a Secret* had asked *Have you ever told your best friend's secret?* or *Have you ever had a friend with anorexia?*, the reader might have answered in his / her mind, *No*; and then lost interest in the topic.

If the writer had asked, *Do you know what anorexia is?*, the reader might have answered *Of course!* and thought that the paragraph topic would be too simple.

10 **Below are several topics and some questions for the first sentence. Tick (✔) the questions that are good. Discuss your choices with a partner.**

Studying in Australia

- ☐ Have you ever been to Australia?
- ☐ Is it more important to be safe or to follow your dream?
- ☐ Where do you want to go to university?
- ☐ Can where you study change your life?

Quitting smoking

- ☐ Is smoking a choice or a disease?
- ☐ Do you smoke?
- ☐ Do you know how to quit smoking?
- ☐ Is it possible to be completely free of an addiction?

Breaking up with a girlfriend

- ☐ Do you have a girlfriend?
- ☐ Do you want to break up with your girlfriend?
- ☐ Can a former girlfriend really become your friend?
- ☐ Is there a kind way to tell someone you no longer love them?

Put it together

11 **Look at the paragraph topics from exercise 9 on page 78, and choose a new one (or choose your own topic about a difficult decision).**

12 **Talk with a partner about your paragraph topic. Write down any good ideas that come from your discussion. If you need more ideas, talk with another partner, or try your favourite method of brainstorming.**

13 **Write your paragraph and then check your writing.**

14 **Exchange papers with a partner.**

- Fill out the Peer Review Form on page 110.
- Talk with your partner and go over each form.

15 **Read your paragraph again and make changes to improve it.**

16 **Hand in the second draft of your paragraph to your teacher.**

12 *Fate or Choice?*

In this unit you will ...

- **write about hopes and plans for the future.**
- **review brainstorming techniques.**
- **review transition expressions.**
- **write a paragraph about the future.**

1 **Look at the pictures. Tell a partner what is happening. What will happen next?**

a

b

2 **Have you ever bought a lottery ticket or entered a draw? Why, or why not? Have you ever won? Share your experiences with a group.**

3 **Read this paragraph to find out if the writer believes in luck.**

> Do You Believe in Luck?
>
> [1.] My parents and friends think that buying lottery tickets is foolish. [2.] They say that ordinary people like me never win, and that it's just a waste of money. [3.] However, I don't agree with this because I know that ordinary people win things. [4.] For example, I've entered draws before, and I've won several times. [5.] I won a T-shirt at my school festival once, and also a gift voucher in a department store. [6.] In addition, my uncle won a free dinner for two people by putting his business card in a draw at a restaurant. [7.] I hope to win a lot of money in the lottery in the future, so I'm going to buy a few lottery tickets. [8.] After all, someone has to win the lottery, and it could be me one day!

4 **Look again at the paragraph on page 80, *Do You Believe in Luck?* Then answer these questions with a partner.**

a. Does the author have the same opinion as you?

b. Which sentence is the topic sentence?

1 ☐   2 ☐   3 ☐

c. Which sentence shows the writer's opinion?

d. Which sentences support the writer's opinion?

e. Which sentences conclude the paragraph?

5 and 6 ☐   6 and 7 ☐   7 and 8 ☐

f. Underline the sentences where the writer talks about the future.

Language focus: Writing about hopes and plans

To talk about your hopes and plans for the future you can use expressions such as *I would like to, I hope to* and *I want to.*

I would like to *be a journalist.*
I hope to *get a job in engineering when I finish university.*
I want to *live a long life, so I never take risks on the road.*

Two verb phrases to write about definite plans for the future are *be going to* and *plan to.*

I'm going to *buy a few lottery tickets.*
I plan to *buy a few lottery tickets.*

5 **Write sentences expressing each of the following peronal wishes or plans. Use a variety of forms.**

a. Tom / race car driver

Tom wants to be a race car driver...........

b. Sandra / politician

....

c. Cooper / married with children in ten years

....

d. Diane / Olympic medal in 2012

....

e. Andrea / a sports car soon

....

f. Write a sentence about a dream / hope that you have.

....

g. Write a sentence about a plan that you have.

....

Brainstorming: Review

6 Work with a partner and do the following.

a. Take turns describing how to do these different types of brainstorming:

1. list
2. word map
3. freewriting
4. discussion
5. list showing order of importance
6. list showing chronological order
7. double list
8. pair interview

b. Explain to your partner which type of brainstorming ...

- is the easiest for you to begin.
- helps you get the most ideas.
- helps you get the most useful ideas.
- is the most difficult for you.
- is your favourite.

7 Choose two or three of these topics. Do a different type of brainstorming for each topic.

a. A career goal
b. Marriage or career?
c. Why I would / wouldn't like to have children
d. An unusual plan for the future
e. A crazy dream?
f. The best place to live
g. A travel plan

8 **Exchange two examples of brainstorming from exercise 7 on page 82 with a partner. Answer these questions.**

a. Did the writer get a lot of ideas?
b. Which brainstorming method gave the most ideas?
c. Which ideas do you think are most interesting for a paragraph?

Writing focus: Review of transition expressions

9 **Work with a partner and do the following.**

- Take turns explaining what the words and expressions below mean, and how they are used.
- Write sentences for at least four of the words / expressions.

Example:
I've nearly finished my English writing textbook, Writing in Paragraphs. **As a result,** *I can write very good paragraphs.*

after
and
as a result
in addition
because
before
but
consequently
for example
however
I think
in my opinion
so
therefore
when

10 **With the same partner, answer these questions about transition expressions.**

a. Why do writers use transition expressions?
b. Should there be a transition expression in each sentence? Why, or why not?
c. Which of the expressions in exercise 9 mean almost the same thing?
d. Choose three expressions and tell about the rules for using commas with them.
e. Which two expressions cannot start a new sentence (in academic writing)?
f. What other transition expressions do you know? Make a list, and share it with another pair or the whole class.

11 **Read this paragraph. With a partner, add transition expressions where needed. Compare your answers in groups. (There could be more than one right answer for each space.)**

Changing my Future

I hope to be a successful artist someday soon. I have been painting since I was a young child [a] .... all my family said I had great talent. [b] .... , I couldn't get a job as an artist or make enough money selling my art. I really want to be an artist, [c] .... I need to make some changes to achieve my dream. First, I plan to study for a graduate degree in Fine Art to learn more about color and to make my paintings more original. [d] .... , I will have more confidence about trying to sell my work. [e] .... , I am going to design a website to show and sell my paintings. If you have dreams, don't wait for fate. You have to do something yourself to achieve your dreams. Going back to school or exploring different business opportunities are just two ways to change your future.

12 **Read the paragraph again to underline any future wishes and plans.**

Put it together

13 **Use one of topics from exercise 7 on page 82 for which you brainstormed ideas.**

14 **Write a paragraph, using transition expressions and some of the future forms you practised. Then check your writing.**

15 **Exchange papers with a partner.**

- Fill out the Peer Review Form on page 111.
- Talk with your partner and go over each form.

16 **Read your paragraph again and make changes to improve it.**

17 **Hand in the second draft of your paragraph to your teacher.**

Additional Materials

Grammar for Writers

This is not a grammar book; this is a writing book. However, good writers should be able to talk about grammar. Then they can talk about their writing. If you know some basic grammar terms, you can learn how to write correct and interesting sentences more easily. You can understand, talk about, and ask questions about the grammatical mistakes you make in your writing, and you can correct them more easily. At the same time, it is important to develop a 'feeling' or intuition about English grammar: you can do this by exposing yourself to English. Read English stories, magazines, and web pages. Listen to English songs; watch English films; have conversations in English. You will be surprised at how these activities also help your writing!

Parts of Speech

➲ **Noun**

A *noun* names something: a person or animal (*teacher, Anne, bird*), a place (*mountain, New York, bedroom*), a thing (*computer, dress, mobile phone*), or idea (*love, honesty, happiness*).

Writers need to think about *noun phrases* in addition to simple nouns. A noun phrase includes the main noun and some words that describe it.

bag (noun)
The bag that my mother gave me (noun phrase)

Note: *Pronouns* (*I, you, he, she, it, we,* and *they*) are words that replace nouns, and are used in the same way.

The topic of your sentences and paragraphs will be a noun or noun phrase.

➲ **Verb**

The *verb* tells about the action or state in the sentence.

He **runs.** *They* **are eating** *dinner.*	(action)
She **seems** *lonely.* *I* **feel** *tired.*	(state)

Verbs change slightly according to who is doing the action (*he runs; they run*) and the tense or time (*he runs every day; he ran yesterday*). We say that a verb must *agree* with the person or thing that the sentence is about.

A *verb phrase* is the main verb (*run*) plus any auxiliary verbs (*does run, is running, has run, could be running*).

Verb phrases show your feelings about your topic. You also use verbs when you write to tell stories and to explain what happened.

Preposition

Prepositions are short words (*at, on, for*) that connect ideas. They tell about time, place, or purpose (reason).

We eat dinner **at** *seven o'clock.* (time)
My book is **on** *the desk.* (place)
She bought a gift **for** *her friend.* (purpose)

A *prepositional phrase* includes a preposition and a noun. The prepositional phrases in the examples above are *at seven o'clock, on the desk* and *for her friend.*

Adding prepositional phrases to your sentences is an easy way to write longer, more detailed sentences.

Adjective

An *adjective* describes, or tells about, a noun. It answers the question *What kind of* or *Which*?

She has a **red** *bag.* (What kind of bag does she have?)
The **small brown** *dog is mine.* (Which dog is yours?)

Adjective phrases – several words – do the same thing. Notice that there can be several adjective phrases for one noun.

She has a bag **from Peru**.
The dog **over there by that tree** *is mine.*

Many adjective phrases are prepositional phrases. Since adjectives and adjective phrases describe nouns, you will often see adjective phrases in noun phrases:

The red bag **with the black handles** *is mine.*

Using adjectives when you write helps you paint a picture of the nouns you are describing. They help your reader to see what you are describing.

Adverb

An *adverb* describes, or tells about, a verb. It answers the questions *Where, When, How, For how long / How often,* and *Why*?

It rained **yesterday.** (When did it rain?)
She eats **slowly**. (How does she eat?)
I **sometimes** *play tennis.* (How often do you play tennis?)

Adverb phrases contain several words. These may also be prepositional phrases. There can be more than one adverb phrase in a sentence.

She went **to the bank to get some money.** (Where did she go? Why did she go there?)

Adverbs add power to your verb phrases. They add more information and support to your ideas.

Use both adjectives and adverbs to make your writing more sophisticated, interesting and accurate.

Article

There are three articles in English: *a*, *an* and *the*. All of the articles signal nouns: *She is* **a friend**; *Would you like* **an apple**?; *Meet me in* **the classroom**. However, not all nouns have articles before them: *I will see you on* **Friday**; *I didn't see that* **film**; *I don't believe in* **magic**. Using English articles correctly takes a lot of practise. Do not be discouraged if you make mistakes with articles while learning to write in English.

Parts of a Sentence

A complete sentence must have a subject and a predicate.

Subject

The subject of a sentence is the person, thing, or idea that the sentence is about. It is always a noun or a noun phrase. In a statement, it usually comes before the verb. To check if your subject agrees with the verb, find the *head noun* – the most basic noun that the sentence is about.

Amy *is my sister.*
She *is my sister.*
The girl *with the long hair is my sister.* (*girl* is the head noun)
The *young* **girl** *with the long hair sitting over there is my sister.* (*girl* is the head noun)

Predicate

The predicate tells what the subject does, what happens to the subject, or how the subject is. The predicate contains at least the verb, and often other words that follow the verb.

Amy **studies.**
Amy **studies English.**
Amy **studies English in her room for several hours every night.**

Finding the subject and predicate of your sentences helps you see whether you have a complete sentence, and whether the subject and verb of your sentence agree.

Punctuation

Here are some common rules for using punctuation in your writing. Of course, this is not a complete list. If you have further questions, check a grammar book or ask your teacher.

Capitalisation

Always capitalise:

- the first word of every sentence.
- days of the week (*Tuesday*) and months of the year (*April*).
- the first letter (only) of the names of people and places (*Bangkok, Ayaka Seo*).
- the main words of a title, but not articles (*a, an, the*) or prepositions (words like *to, of, for*) or conjunctions (*and, but*), unless they are the first word in the title: *The Three Things I Do in the Morning.*

Full stop (.)

A full stop comes at the end of a statement:
An electronic dictionary is more convenient than a paper one.

If the sentence ends with an abbreviation, don't use more than one full stop:
RIGHT: *My mother just finished her Ph.D.*
WRONG: *My mother just finished her Ph.D..*

Comma (,)

Use a comma to separate a series of three or more items. However, only use a comma between the last two items and *and* if they are long.
I take a dictionary, a notebook and some paper to class every day.
I spent last week swimming in the pool, lying in the sun, and reading all about love and adventure.

Use a comma before words like *and, but, or,* and *so* to separate two parts of a sentence that each have a subject and a verb.
She needed some work experience, so she got a part-time job.
He did not study at all, but he still got an 87 on the test.

Use a comma after an introductory word or expression, such as *However, Therefore,* and *In conclusion*:
However, the high price of electric cars means that most people cannot afford one.

Quotation marks (' ')

Use quotation marks when you type or write the title of a book or film:
'Hamlet' was written by Shakespeare.

When you use a word processor, you can use italics instead:
Hamlet was written by Shakespeare.

Use quotation marks to show the exact words someone spoke or wrote:
The professor announced, 'We're going to have an exam next week.'
Shakespeare wrote, 'All the world's a stage.'

Do not use quotation marks if you're reporting what another person said:
The professor said that we should study hard this week.

Punctuation when using quotation marks

If you are using expressions like *he said* or *the girl remarked* after the quotation, then use a comma and not a full stop at the end of the quoted sentence:
'We're going to have an exam next week,' announced the professor.

Use a full stop if the quoted sentence comes at the end:
The professor announced, 'We're going to have an exam next week.'

Notice how a comma is used after *announced*, above, to introduce the quotation.

Quotation marks and capitalisation

Capitalise the first letter of the word that begins a quotation. However, if an expression like *she said* interrupts the quotation and divides the sentence, then do not capitalise the first word of the part that finishes the quotation:
'Next week,' said the professor, 'we are going to have an exam.'

The comma after *week* separates the quotation from the rest of the sentence.

Use a capital letter only if the second part is a new, complete sentence:
'We'll have an exam next week,' explained the teacher. 'It will take thirty minutes.'

Advice for academic writing

The following are not usually used in academic writing, although they are fine in informal situations, such as letters to your friends.

- Brackets that give information which is not part of your main sentence:
  Mobile phones are useful (and besides, I think they look great).
  If your idea is important, it should be in a sentence of its own. If it is not important, it should not be in your paper.
- The abbreviation *etc.* to continue a list. Instead, use a phrase like *such as* in your sentence:
  Students in my university come from countries such as China, India and Australia.
- Exclamation marks (!). Instead, write strong sentences with plenty of details to show your reader your feelings:
  Angel Falls is one of the most spectacular natural wonders you will ever see.
- An ellipsis (...) at the end of a sentence, to show that the sentence is not finished:
  The professor said that I should study hard, so ...
  Instead, finish your sentence:
  The professor said that I should study hard, so I should not go to the party tonight.

Irregular Verb List

Here is a list of common irregular verbs in English with their past tense (*I* **took** *the test*) and past participle (*I have* **taken** *three tests this month*).

Infinitive	Simple past	Past participle
be	was/were	been
beat	beat	beaten
become	became	become
begin	began	begun
bend	bent	bent
bet	bet	bet
bite	bit	bitten
blow	blew	blown
break	broke	broken
bring	brought	brought
build	built	built
burn	burnt/burned	burnt/burned
burst	burst	burst
buy	bought	bought
can	could	(been able)
catch	caught	caught
choose	chose	chosen
come	came	come
cost	cost	cost
cut	cut	cut
deal	dealt	dealt
do	did	done
draw	drew	drawn
dream	dreamt/dreamed	dreamt/dreamed
drink	drank	drunk
drive	drove	driven
eat	ate	eaten
fall	fell	fallen
feed	fed	fed
feel	felt	felt
fight	fought	fought
find	found	found
fly	flew	flown
forget	forgot	forgotten
forgive	forgave	forgiven
freeze	froze	frozen
get	got	got
give	gave	given
go	went	gone
grow	grew	grown
hang	hung/hanged	hung/hanged
have	had	had
hear	heard	heard
hide	hid	hidden
hit	hit	hit
hold	held	held
hurt	hurt	hurt
keep	kept	kept
kneel	knelt	knelt
know	knew	known
lay	laid	laid
lead	led	led
learn	learnt/learned	learnt/learned
leave	left	left
lend	lent	lent
let	let	let

Infinitive	Simple past	Past participle
lie	lay	lain
light	lit/lighted	lit/lighted
lose	lost	lost
make	made	made
mean	meant	meant
meet	met	met
must	had to	(had to)
pay	paid	paid
put	put	put
read	read \red\	read \red\
ride	rode	ridden
ring	rang	rung
rise	rose	risen
run	ran	run
say	said	said
see	saw	seen
sell	sold	sold
send	sent	sent
set	set	set
shake	shook	shaken
shine	shone/shined	shone/shined
shoot	shot	shot
show	showed	shown
shrink	shrank	shrunk
shut	shut	shut
sing	sang	sung
sink	sank	sunk
sit	sat	sat
sleep	slept	slept
slide	slid	slid
smell	smelt/smelled	smelt/smelled
speak	spoke	spoken
spell	spelt/spelled	spelt/spelled
spend	spent	spent
spill	spilt/spilled	spilt/spilled
split	split	split
spoil	spoilt/spoiled	spoilt/spoiled
spread	spread	spread
stand	stood	stood
steal	stole	stolen
stick	stuck	stuck
swear	swore	sworn
swell	swelled	swollen/swelled
swim	swam	swum
take	took	taken
teach	taught	taught
tear	tore	torn
tell	told	told
think	thought	thought
throw	threw	thrown
understand	understood	understood
wake	woke	woken
wear	wore	worn
win	won	won
write	wrote	written

Sample paragraph: Brainstorming

Assignment: Write a paragraph about a person who is important to you. Explain why that person is special. Use a word map to brainstorm ideas, edit your map, and then write your first draft. Then exchange papers with a classmate and fill out a Peer Review Form. After you receive your classmate's form, write a second draft using ideas from your classmate and your own ideas.

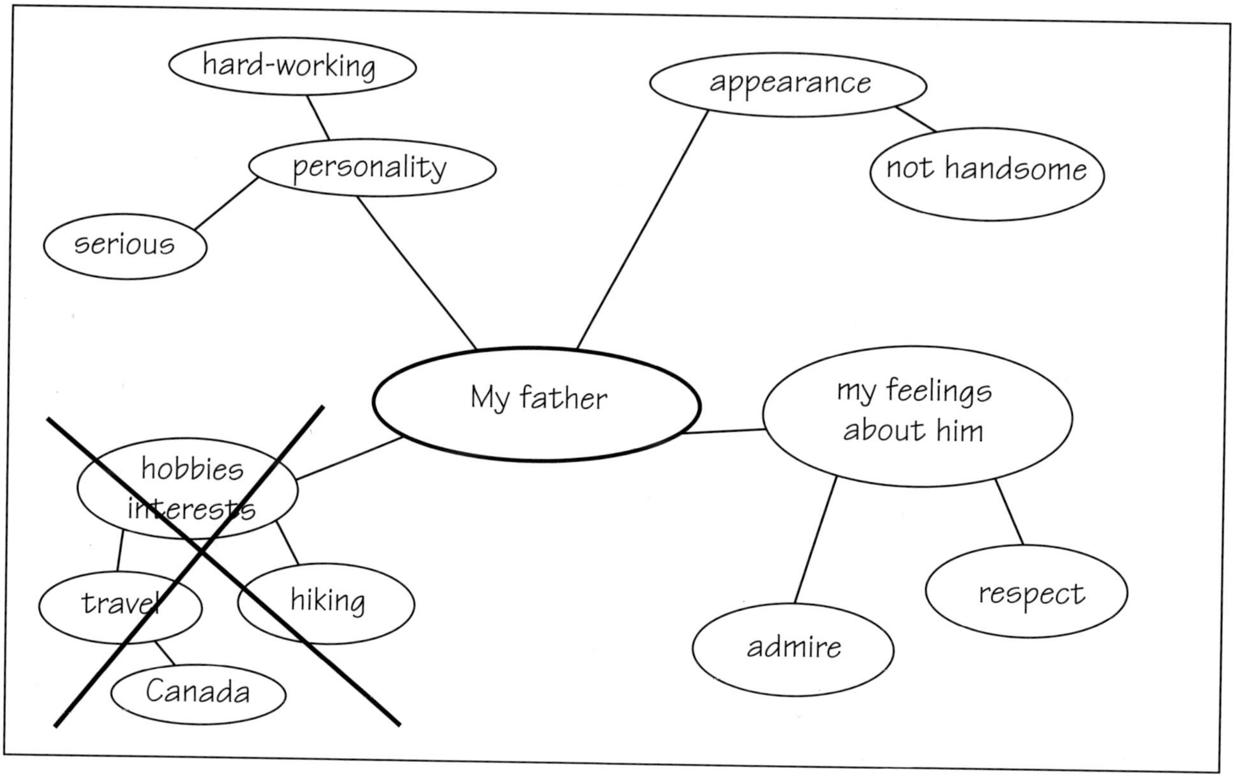

Sample paragraph: First draft

Kensaku Isagawa
11 May, 2004
Writing Class
Instructor: Carlos Islam

1st Draft

I admire many things about my father. He does not have any special qualities. He would be easy to overlook because he is not special. He is a good person. I get bored when I work with him. He has strong opinions, and he is tough and generous to other peoples. He always looks at the future. He never regrets something. I learned a lot from him.

Peer Review Form

Writer's name: Kensaku Isagawa

Reviewer's name: Yumiko Hara

Title: ?

Date: 12 May, 2005

1. What is the topic of the paragraph? What is the writer's opinion about that topic?
   Topic = Ken's father Opinion = Ken admires his father
2. Look at the word map. Were any ideas crossed out? Why, do you think?
   Yes, he crossed out "hobbies." I don't know why, but maybe there were too many ideas for one paragraph. "Hobbies" is not why he admires his father, I guess.
3. Read the paragraph again. What is the topic sentence? Write it here.
   I admire many things about my father.
   Circle the topic and underline the main idea.
4. How many supporting sentences are there?
   seven
5. Is there a concluding sentence? If so, what does it do (for example, restate the topic sentence, give advice, make a prediction, offer a final comment)?
   Yes, it offers a final comment.
6. Which sentence is your favourite? Write it here.
   He has strong opinions, and he is tough and generous to other peoples.
7. Do you have any questions or comments for the writer?
   This is interesting. I want to know more about your father. Also, I think it is better to be specific. Why is he a 'good' person and why isn't he 'special'?
   I think the sentence, 'I get bored when I work with him' is not connected to your idea. The concluding sentence would be stronger if you said what you learned from your father, or if said something like, 'I hope I can be like my father when I have children.' Also, I want to know what doesn't he regret? Can you tell me examples? What have you learned from him?

Sample paragraph: Final draft

Kensaku Isagawa
15 May, 2005
Writing Class
Instructor: Carlos Islam

I Respect My Father

I admire many things about my father, but he does not have any special qualities. He would be easy to overlook because he is not outstandingly handsome or striking in appearance. However, he is a careful, serious, and hard working person. He has strong opinions, and he is tough and generous to other people. He always looks to the future. He never regrets anything. I think I learned a lot from him.

Answer Key

Introduction

Layout / Formatting

1a

a. 4 b. 2 c. 6 d. 1 e. 5 f. 3

1b

a. It is in a clear, easy-to-read font and all in one colour – black.

2

a.
1. Karen Chou
2. English Writing 1
3. Professor Miller
4. School Uniforms Are Good

b.
1. Sebastian Mitchell
2. Students Should Choose Their Own Clothes
3. school uniforms
4. It's the second time the student has written this assignment.
5. 5 September, 2004

Process writing

3

a. 'Process writing' means writing in several stages (steps).
b. Before you begin to write, you should get some ideas.
c. Your teacher may ask you to read a classmate's paper and answer some questions about it. This is because you can learn a lot by reading your classmate's assignment.
d. Your teacher may ask you to write another draft. This is because you can make your paper better by making some changes.
e. Before you hand in your paper for a grade, you should check it carefully.

1 Beginning to Work

1

Answers will vary.

3

b. Working and studying at the same time

5

Sentence 1

6

b. They give examples.

Writing focus: What is a sentence?

8

b. we love writing in English
c. his friends are not in his class

Language focus: Capital letters and final punctuation

9

b. Computer science is a useful subject.
c. I don't like working with people.
d. Many students can't find a job easily.
e. Are more women working after university?
f. My first job was a wonderful experience.

10

a. (needs a subject and a verb)
b. We love writing in English.
c. His friends are not in his class.
d. (needs a verb)
e. (needs a subject and a verb)
f. (needs a subject)
g. (needs a subject)

Writing focus: What is a paragraph?

11

a. strong: there is a clear topic sentence; the supporting sentences are all about the same topic
b. weak: some sentences say the same thing
c. weak: there is no topic sentence. To demonstrate this, ask the class what the paragraph is about (copying a song from a computer's hard disk to a CD). Then ask students which sentence states this directly – there isn't one.

d. strong: there is a clear topic sentence; the supporting sentences are all about the same topic
e. weak: there is no topic sentence; there are not enough sentences
f. weak: the sentences are not all about the same topic

12
c. What my first job taught me

13
(sentences that are not related to the topic)
3. My best friend had a more exciting job.
6. Now at weekends I like to sleep late.
8. My parents' house was very clean, too.

14
a. C b. U c. U d. C e. C f. U g. U

Put it together

15
(unconnected sentences)
I was the youngest person in my school class.
I took a business class at university that was very good.
University tuition in the U.S. is more expensive than in many other countries.
Some universities help their graduates find jobs after graduation.

16

> Part-time Jobs are Good for Students
>
> Having a part-time job is a valuable experience for secondary school students. They can learn many things that are not usually taught in a classroom. For example, they can learn how to work with older people. They also get experience with the business world. Having a part-time job gives students a sense of independence. They can also earn money to use for university. Education is more than just school subjects. Learning about the real world is also important.

2 Giving and Receiving Presents

2
a. 3 b. 2 c. 1

3
b. (Snowboarding) is my <u>favourite winter sport</u>.

c. The last (CD) I bought <u>changed my life</u>.

d. There are three reasons why my (mobile phone) is <u>useful</u>.

e. (Reading novels,) such as the Harry Potter stories, <u>can help students improve their English</u>.

f. My (part-time job) <u>taught me several new skills</u>.

g. (Disneyland) was a <u>great place for our family holiday</u>.

4
The first sentence is the topic sentence.

(Choosing a birthday present) for a friend or family member is fun, but it <u>can be difficult</u>.

5
b. (1.)
2. It's too broad.
c. 1. There is more than one main idea.
(2.)
d. (1.)
2. It's too narrow.
e. 1. It's too broad.
(2.)
f. 1. It's too broad.
(2.)
g. 1. There is no main idea or opinion.
(2.)

6
Answers will vary.

Language focus: Using and and but to join sentences

7
- The sentences are similar because they have the same information.
- They have different punctuation; the examples in 1. are two sentences, and the examples in 2. are one sentence.

- The examples in 2. are more fluent and sound more sophisticated. (This information is explained just after the exercise, so if students didn't figure it out while doing the exercise, go ahead to the next section.)
- In 7c the actions are similar because neither of them sent a present.
- In 7b the contrast is that the person likes flowers but not chocolates.

8

1. Choosing a birthday present for a friend or family member is fun, but it can be difficult.
2. The present should be personal and has to be thoughtful.
5. He is standing with his mother and father (my grandparents) in front of their house, and he looks happy.

9

a. but
b. and
c. and
d. but
e. but

Language focus: Punctuation

10

b. Ahmed speaks English very well, and he enjoys his classes.
c. Yoshi studies hard, but he doesn't get good grades.
d. In Asia, most people eat rice for breakfast, but in Canada, they have cereal.
e. Morocco has lovely mountains and beautiful beaches.
f. Spanish is spoken in most of South America, but Portuguese is spoken in Brazil.
g. Presents are difficult to choose but fun to give.
h. Noodles are easy to cook and are popular in many countries.

3 A Favourite Place

2

a. 2
b. 3. Explain the topic sentence by giving more information.

3

look	sound	smell	feel
dark	exciting	fragrant	dry
exciting	friendly	spicy	humid
friendly	loud	sweet	relaxed
green	musical		sharp
relaxed	quiet		soft
sharp			warm
soft			
spicy			
sweet			
warm			

4

look	sound	smell	feel
fresh (water)	noisy (beach)	salty (air)	hot (air)
tired	pleasant (noise)	sweet (air)	cool (water)
white (sand)			wet (water)
soft (sand)			fresh (water)
peaceful			tired
relaxed			soft (sand)
			peaceful
			relaxed

5

(ideas not used)
air – dry, windy
water – cold
can't windsurf
good snack food
beach umbrellas / expensive to rent
too far away
sounds – ocean waves
taste – salt water tastes bad

Writing focus: Combining sentences containing adjectives

9

<u>Similarities:</u> The title, topic, and ideas are the same.
<u>Differences:</u> In the second paragraph some sentences have been combined, and there is more variety in sentence type.
While each paragraph is grammatically correct, the second one sounds more natural and more sophisticated.

10

3. The air is hot, but the water is cool, wet, and fresh.
4. First, I enjoy swimming and surfing in the sea.
5. When I am tired, I come out and lie on the beach.
6. The sand is soft and white.
7. The beach is noisy with seagulls and children laughing, but it's a pleasant noise.

9. The air smells salty from the sea and sweet from everybody's sun cream.
10. I feel peaceful and relaxed.

11
a. Charles is interesting, but a little strange.
b. The river was deep, wide, and cold.
c. Our teacher is strict but fair.
d. July was hot and humid.
e. Kim is my best friend because she is kind, smart, and funny.
f. The food in that restaurant is delicious but expensive.

4 An Exceptional Person

2
The third person is most like Jack.

a. The first sentence.
Jack Collins is the most amazing person I have ever met.
b. 8, 9
c. 6, 7

3
b. life
c. He (Jack Collins)
d. Jack
e. He (Jack)
f. personality

4
secondary school (describes *students*)

Writing focus: Concluding sentences

8
a. 1 (restate)
b. 3 (predict)
c. 4 (suggest or advise)
d. 2 (summarise)

11
Sentence 3: it adds supporting detail, but does not restate, summarise, suggest or advise, or predict.

Language focus: Punctuation

14
David Beckham: a person's name
England: a place name
Manchester United: a team's name
Spain: a place name
Real Madrid: a team's name
Beckham (two times): a person's name
England: a place name
World Cup: the name of a specific thing (like *the Olympics*)
Brazil: a place name

15
a. David Beckham married Victoria Adams, who was a singer with the Spice Girls, a pop group in the 1990s.
b. Beckham learned to speak Spanish because he moved to Madrid.
c. In March 1999, David and Victoria had their first son.
d. The Beckhams now have three children, called Brooklyn, Romeo and Cruz.
e. Romeo was born in September 2002 and Cruz was born in February 2005.
f. There is a funny film called 'Bend it Like Beckham,' which is about one of David Beckham's fans.

Put it together

16
a. 4 b. 1 c. 6 d. 5 e. 2 f. 3

5 Trends and Fashions

3
a. 3
b. 3. Explain the topic sentence by giving more information.
c. 1, 4

Language focus: Vocabulary review

4

people	places	things
busy	busy	difficult
difficult	humid	convenient
optimistic	convenient	exciting
shy	exciting	noisy
exciting	noisy	popular
popular	popular	spicy
friendly	comfortable	comfortable
peaceful	friendly	salty
	peaceful	valuable

Paragraph review

10
a. S b. S c. C d. T e. S f. S

11

My New Mountain Bike
Mountain bikes are really popular where I live. Everybody has one. So, I bought a bike last week for £150 in a second-hand bike sale. The bike is one year old but looks new. The colors are bright red, white, and dark blue. It looks like a bike you can ride on very rough mountains and over rocks. It's a great bike, and I'm going to have a lot of fun on it.

12

- Brainstorming; getting ideas.
- Writing a first draft; beginning to write.
- Checking work; editing.
- Peer reviewing; checking someone else's work; having someone else check your work.
- Writing a second draft; making some changes; editing; rewriting.
- Handing in the paper; finishing.

Writing focus: Peer reviewing

13

a. ✔
b. ✗ It isn't kind.
c. ✔
d. ✔
e. ✔
f. ✗ It isn't clear; it isn't useful.
g. ✗ It isn't kind; it isn't clear; it isn't useful.
h. ✔
i. ✔
j. ✗ It isn't useful.
k. ✔

6 White Lies

1

b.

3

a. The first sentence, 'White lies are not always bad.'
b. 3. It makes a suggestion.
c. 2. They give examples.

Language focus: Giving an opinion

4

b. Good teachers don't give too much homework. <u>O</u>
Our teacher gave us homework last week. <u>F</u>
c. Keanu Reeves is a good actor. <u>O</u>
Keanu Reeves starred in the *Matrix* films. <u>F</u>
d. Many teens carry mobile phones these days. <u>F</u>
Mobile phones are very convenient. <u>O</u>
e. All students have to wear a uniform at my school. <u>F</u>
Our school uniforms are not very comfortable. <u>O</u>
f. I don't believe that wearing the latest fashions is important. <u>O</u>
My favourite clothes are all black. <u>F</u>

Writing focus: Supporting sentences with opinions and examples

7

<u>Opinions:</u> Sentences: 1, 3, 6
<u>Examples:</u> Sentences: 2, 4, 5
<u>Both:</u> Sentences: 4, 5

8

a. O b. E c. O d. O e. E f. E g. E

9

a. 1; 4 b. sentences 3 and 7

7 Explanations and Excuses

3

a. W b. T c. T d. W e. T

Language focus: Giving explanations

4

5. He's my best friend [cause], so I had to go to his party [result].
7. I was too tired to write it again [result] because it was very late [cause].
9. She said, 'You had two weeks to do the assignment [cause], so there are no excuses [result].'

5

b. We played badly, so we lost the football match. / We lost the football match because we played badly.
c. I didn't study hard, so I failed the test. / I failed the test because I didn't study hard.
d. My alarm clock didn't work, so I was late for the meeting. / I was late for the meeting because my alarm clock didn't work.
e. I am shy, so I don't have a girlfriend. / I don't have a girlfriend because I am shy.
f. I'm tired, so I won't go to the party. / I won't go to the party because I'm tired.

Language focus: Starting with because

6

Sentences with the *because* clause second don't need a comma. Sentences with the *because* clause first need a comma after the first clause.

7

b. I don't exercise because I am too busy. / Because I am too busy, I don't exercise.
c. I go to bed late because I have too much homework. / Because I have too much homework, I go to bed late.
d. I can't give up smoking because I will put on weight. / Because I will put on weight, I can't give up smoking.
e. I lost my friend's book because I was careless. / Because I was careless, I lost my friend's book.
f. I'm not going to go to the beach because I have to take an exam. / Because I have to take an exam, I'm not going to go to the beach.

8

a. Christmas cards (why I don't send Christmas cards)
b. four (plus one that is crossed out)
c. They were not as important or interesting as the other ideas.

9

Topic sentence:
However, I don't send Christmas cards. *or*
However, I (almost) never send Christmas cards.
a. so
b. because
c. Because

8 Problems

3

a. 1. Talking to friends and classmates is easy for a lot of teenage boys, but talking to parents is more difficult.
b. 2 (It makes a prediction.) and 3 (It makes a suggestion.)
c. 1. No. It is about his father, but is not related to the main idea of communication.
   2. Yes. This could be an explanation for why the writer's father doesn't talk to his son.
   3. Yes. This could be another reason why the writer's father doesn't talk to his son.
   4. No. It is not relevant to the topic.
   5. No. It is not relevant to the topic.
   6. Yes. This could be a good concluding sentence.

Language focus: Want to, would like to, have to

4

2. Many teenage boys would like to talk to their fathers about their feelings, but they don't know how.
3. Sons often want to know how their fathers feel about them.
4. For example, I would like my father to say that he is proud of me.
6. He only wants to talk about sports or my schoolwork.
7. Parents have to talk to their kids about their feelings, or their children will feel lonely at home.

5

a. has to
b. wants to / would like to
c. want to / would like to
d. wanted to; had to
e. have to
f. want to / would like to; (will) have to
g. want to / would like to

Writing focus: Order of supporting ideas

7 & 8

The two details not used were: got better grades in Spanish; best friend (Linda) was in the same class.

9

1 Last year I ran the London marathon, and it was the hardest thing I've ever done.
2 I had to spend about six months training for the marathon before it even started.
3 On the day of the marathon, I had to get up at 5 a.m. and get to the starting line. It was cold, and everyone was very tired.
4 The beginning of the race was a lot of fun because the crowd was cheering and the sun was shining.
5 After thirteen miles, the middle of the marathon, my legs began to hurt and I started to get bored.
6 The twenty-mile point was the worst because I had been running for three hours, I was hungry, and I was in a lot of pain.
7 When I crossed the finish line, I could hardly walk and I felt sick.
8 Next year, I would like to watch the marathon but not run it.

11

c. To make the reader interested in the topic.

9 Strange Stories

2

a. 1
b. 1
c. 2
d. Yes, it is, because it sums up the result of the story. Concluding sentences for narrative paragraphs will often give some kind of final comment or result. If students feel that sentence 11 is a concluding sentence but cannot explain why, guide them to this idea by asking them what the ends of stories usually tell.

Language focus: Using time expressions

3

b. after
c. when
d. before
e. before
f. When

5

a. before
b. after
c. When (*After* is also possible, though *When* would be the first choice in English)

Writing focus: Narrative paragraphs

8

a. 4 middle of the story
b. 1 background information
c. 5 end of the story
d. 3 middle of the story
e. 2 beginning of the story

9

<u>A Fright in the Forest</u>

a. 3 from the middle of the story
b. 1 background information
c. 4 from the end of the story
d. 2 from the beginning of the story

<u>A Strange Day in Class</u>

a. 1 background information
b. 4 from the end of the story
c. 2 from the beginning of the story
d. 3 from the middle of the story

10 Differences

3

a. Three differences: secondary school was small, but university was big; at school there were the same number of boys and girls in the classes, but at university there were only a few other girls; at school the teacher told students what to study, but at university the writer had to do a lot of reading and learning alone.
b. Answers will vary (however, the writer does say she enjoyed university more).
c. Answers will vary.

Brainstorming: Double lists

5

The writer prefers winter which he/she says is 'even more spectacular'.

6

<u>Summer</u>	<u>Winter</u>
warm	snow
watching wildlife	beautiful scenery
hiking in mountains	tobogganing / dogsledding
climbing	snowboarding / skiing
	French cafés
	tapas bars

Language focus: However / whereas

8

<u>University Life</u>	<u>Winter in the Pyrenees</u>
Sentences 3 and 8	Sentence 5

9

a. Skiing is a popular winter sport. However, many young people prefer snowboarding.
b. Whereas my science class has over 300 people in it, my English seminar has just 12.
c. Dogs are more faithful, whereas cats are more independent.
d. Cars are faster. However, I'd rather ride my bicycle.
e. I have a huge video tape collection. However, DVDs are more common these days.
f. Answers will vary.

11 Difficult Decisions

2

a. 1 My friend thought she was fat.
   2 My friend wouldn't eat any food.
b. 2 I hesitated to tell her parents.
   1 I thought she might get angry.

c. 2 Her parents made sure she ate all her meals.
   1 I told her parents her secret.
d. 2 My friend is healthier now.
   1 Her parents and the psychologist helped her.

3
c.

4
b.

Language focus: Cause and effect

5
a. The comma is used after the words *as a result*, *consequently*, or *therefore* when they begin a sentence.
b. The comma is used before the word *and*.

6
a. I wanted to travel for a year after school. Consequently, I didn't go to university right away.
b. My parents needed help in their restaurant. As a result, I moved back home and worked for them.
c. Cars are very convenient, and consequently, people use them more than they should.
d. My parents didn't want me to date before I finished school. Therefore, I told Tim that I couldn't go out with him.
e. Our school didn't have a lot of money, and consequently the administration decided to cancel some after-school clubs.
f. My friends complained that it was hard to communicate with me. As a result, I bought a mobile phone, even though I don't like them.

Writing focus: Using questions to catch attention

10
<u>Studying in Australia</u>
Is it more important to be safe or to follow your dream?
Can where you study change your life?

<u>Quitting smoking</u>
Is smoking a choice or a disease?
Is it possible to be completely free of an addiction?

<u>Breaking up with a girlfriend</u>
Can a former girlfriend really become your friend?
Is there a kind way to tell someone you no longer love them?

12 Fate or Choice?

4
a. Answers will vary.
b. 3
c. 3
d. 4, 5 and 6
e. 7 and 8
f. 7 and 8

Language focus: Writing about hopes and plans

5
b. Sandra would like to be a politician.
c. Cooper wants to be married with children in ten years.
d. Diane hopes to win an Olympic medal in 2012.
e. Andrea would like to buy a sports car soon.
f. / g. Answers will vary.

Writing focus: Review of transition expressions

10
a. *Suggested answer*: Writers use transition expressions to show connections between ideas, to make their writing more connected, and to make their writing easier for a reader to understand.
b. No, because it will sound unnatural.
c. *and*; *in addition*
   as a result; consequently; therefore; so
   I think; in my opinion
   but; however
d. Answers will vary.
e. *and; but* (instead, use *In addition* and *However*)
f. Answers will vary.

11
a. and
b. However
c. but
d. As a result / Consequently / Therefore
e. In addition

12
I hope to be a successful artist someday soon.
I really want to be an artist, (but) I need to make some changes to achieve my dream.
First, I plan to study for a graduate degree in Fine Art …
(In addition), I am going to design a website to show and sell my paintings.
You have to do something yourself to achieve your dreams.

Photocopiable Materials

Peer Review Form – Unit 5

Writer's name: ....

Reviewer's name: ....

Title: ....

Date: ....

1. What is the topic of the paragraph? What is the writer's opinion about that topic?

2. Look at the freewriting. Is it long or short? Have any ideas been crossed out? Why, do you think?

3. Read the paragraph again. What is the topic sentence? Write it here.

....

....

Circle the topic and underline the main idea.

4. How many supporting sentences are there?

5. Is there a concluding sentence? If so, what does it do (for example, restate the topic sentence, give advice, make a prediction, offer a final comment)?

6. Does the paragraph have these things?

	yes	no
• writer's name and date		
• paragraph title		
• descriptive adjectives		
• some sentences or adjectives combined with *and*		
• some sentences or adjectives combined with *but*		

7. Do you have any questions or comments for the writer?

PHOTOCOPIABLE

Peer Review Form – Unit 6

Writer's name: ....

Reviewer's name: ....

Title: ....

Date: ....

1. What is the topic of the paragraph? What is the writer's opinion about that topic?

2. Read the paragraph again. What is the topic sentence? Write it here.

   ....

   ....

   Circle the topic and underline the main idea.

3. How many supporting sentences are there?

4. Underline supporting sentences that state an opinion.

5. Double underline sentences that support an opinion.

6. How many sentences state facts?

7. Is there a concluding sentence? If so, what does it do (for example, restate the topic sentence, make a prediction, give a suggestion)?

8. Which sentence is your favourite? Write it here.

   ....

   ....

9. Do you have any questions or comments for the writer?

PHOTOCOPIABLE

Peer Review Form – Unit 7

Writer's name: ....

Reviewer's name: ....

Title: ....

Date: ....

1. What is the topic of the paragraph?

2. Look at the brainstorming.

a. What kind of brainstorming did the writer use?

b. Was the brainstorming edited?

c. Do you think that method helped the writer think of a lot of ideas?

3. Read the paragraph again.

a. What do you think about the writer's explanation or excuse?

b. Would you make the same choice, do you think? Why, or why not?

4. Underline the topic sentence.

5. Did the writer combine any sentences with *so* or *because?* If so, write them here.

....

....

....

6. Which sentence is your favourite? Write it here.

....

....

7. Do you have any questions or comments for the writer?

Peer Review Form – Unit 8

Writer's name: ....

Reviewer's name: ....

Title: ....

Date: ....

1. What is the topic? What problem does the writer explain?

2. Look at the writer's list.

a. Which idea do you think is the most important?

b. Were any ideas crossed out? Why, do you think?

c. Did the writer number his / her ideas in order of importance?

3. Read the paragraph again. What is the topic sentence? Write it here.

....

....

Circle the topic and underline the main idea.

4. How many supporting sentences are there?

5. Is there a concluding sentence? If so, what does it do?

6. Write the last supporting sentence. Is it the most important supporting idea?

....

....

7. Does the paragraph have these things?

8. Do you have any questions or comments for the writer?

Peer Review Form – Unit 9

Writer's name: ....

Reviewer's name: ....

Title: ....

Date: ....

1. What is the topic of the paragraph?

2. Write one or two words to describe the feeling or mood of the narrative (for example, *scary*, *strange*, *happy*, *sad*).

3. Look at the brainstorming.

a. What kind of brainstorming did the writer use?

b. Was the brainstorming edited?

c. Do you think that method helped the writer think of a lot of ideas?

4. Read the paragraph again. Make a list of the main events, in the order they happened.

5. Is there a concluding sentence? If so, what does it do?

6. Which sentence is your favourite? Write it here.

....

....

7. Does the paragraph have these things?

8. Do you have any questions or comments for the writer?

PHOTOCOPIABLE

Peer Review Form – Unit 10

Writer's name: ....

Reviewer's name: ....

Title: ....

Date: ....

1. What two things is the writer comparing? What is the writer's opinion about each of the things?

2. Look at the double list the writer used to brainstorm.

a. Was it long or short?

b. Which ideas were used?

c. Were they the most interesting to you?

3. Read the paragraph again. What is the topic sentence? Write it here.

....

....

Circle the topic and underline the main idea.

4. How many supporting sentences are there?

5. Is there a concluding sentence? If so, what does it do?

6. Does the paragraph have these things?

	yes	**no**
• point-by-point style		
• block style		
• two ideas joined using *whereas*		
• two ideas joined using *however*		

7. Do you have any questions or comments for the writer?

Peer Review Form – Unit 11

Writer's name: ....

Reviewer's name: ....

Title: ....

Date: ....

1. What is the difficult decision the writer made? Why was it difficult?

2. What is the topic sentence? Write it here.

....

....

3. Did the writer begin with a question? If so, how did you answer it?

4. Read the paragraph again. Underline the words and expressions the writer used to link sentences and ideas (such as *and, but, because, so, therefore, as a result, consequently*).

Do you think the writer used commas correctly in those sentences? If you are not sure, make a star (*) next to the sentence.

5. Was it easy to understand the paragraph? Were all the events told in a logical order?

6. Is there a concluding sentence? If so, what does it do?

7. Which sentence is your favourite? Write it here.

....

....

8. Do you have any questions or comments for the writer?

PHOTOCOPIABLE

Peer Review Form – Unit 12

Writer's name: ....

Reviewer's name: ....

Title: ....

Date: ....

1. What is the topic of the paragraph? What is the writer's opinion about that topic?

2. Look at the brainstorming.

a. Would you have used a different technique? Why, or why not?

b. Did the writer get a lot of ideas from the brainstorming?

3. Read the paragraph again. What does the writer hope or desire for the future?

4. How many supporting sentences are there?

5. Do the supporting sentences include any of these things?

	yes	no
• transition expressions		
• facts		
• opinions		
• examples		

6. Is there a concluding sentence? If so, what does it do?

7. Which sentence is your favourite? Write it here.

....

....

8. Do you have any questions or comments for the writer?

Writing Survey

This survey gives students a chance to reflect on their own experiences with and attitudes towards writing, and to share their experiences with classmates. You could do this at the start of the course as an ice-breaker and to get some ideas about how students feel about writing and what they hope to learn on the course.

- Make one copy of the survey for each student in the class.
- Put students in pairs or small groups to discuss the questions and then conduct a class feedback session.
- Alternatively, have them write out answers as homework to hand in.

Writing Survey

1. Answer the questions.

a. What types of writing do you do in your native language at least once a month? Add to the list.

❒ letters ❒ lists ❒ e-mail ❒ diary

❒ compositions ❒ .... ❒ .... ❒ ....

b. What type of writing is the most enjoyable? What type is the least enjoyable? Why?

c. How often do you write in English? What do you write in English?

d. Will you write in English in the future? What kinds of things will you write?

e. When you write:

	yes	no
Do you write with pencil and paper?	❒	❒
Do you use a computer?	❒	❒
Do you use a dictionary?	❒	❒
Do you make notes before you write?	❒	❒
Do you write your paper in your native language first?	❒	❒
Do you write your paper more than once?	❒	❒

f. How easy are these things when you write in English? Circle the most appropriate number. (1 = very easy, 2 = somewhat easy, 3 = somewhat challenging, 4 = very challenging)

grammar	1	2	3	4
expressing myself	1	2	3	4
vocabulary / finding the right word	1	2	3	4
getting ideas	1	2	3	4
writing something interesting	1	2	3	4

g. What do you hope to learn from this class?

2. Share your answers with a partner or small group.

Macmillan Education
Between Towns Road, Oxford OX4 3PP
A division of Macmillan Publishers Limited
Companies and representatives throughout the world

ISBN-13: 978-1-4050-9586-0
ISBN-10: 1-4050-9586-5

First published 2006

Designed by Amanda Easter Design Ltd

Illustrated by Jackson Graham, Sophie Grillet, Stuart Perry and Peter Harper
Cover design by Andrew Oliver
Cover illustration/photograph: Alamy images

Authors' acknowledgements
Thanks to students in the Intensive English Institute at The University of Maine, especially Kensaku Isagawa, who kindly helped pilot many of the exercises in the book and provided helpful comments and suggestions. Special thanks to Tony Garside, Helen Holwill, and David Williamson.

The publishers would like to thank the following for their assistance in the development of this course (in alphabetical order):
Stuart Bowie, Kevin Cleary, Chris Cottam, Clyde Fowle, Takashi Hata, Jeong-Sook Lee, Pearl Lin, Steve Maginn, David Parker, Thawatchai Pattarawongvisut, Cristina Roberts, Gordon Robson, Satoshi Saito, Maria-Luiza Santos, Lucy Torres, Sandra Wu, Jin-Soo Yoon

The authors and publishers would like to thank the following for permission to reproduce their photographs: Alamy / Brand x p17(l), Alamy / Alexander Caminada p17(r); Corbis / Reg Charity p25, Corbis / Mike Chew p14, Corbis / Anne W. Krause p84, Corbis / Jose Luis Pelaez p29(c), Corbis / Patrick Ward p20, Corbis / Jeff Zaruba p44; Empics p59; Getty pp6, 31, 63, Getty / Image State p29(a), Getty / Stone pp13, 62, Getty / Taxi p55; Image Source p29(d); Zefa pp29(b), 34, 45.

Whilst every effort has been made to locate the owners of copyright material in this book, there may have been some cases when the publishers have been unable to contact the owners. We should be grateful to hear from anyone who recognises copyright material and who is unacknowledged. We shall be pleased to make the necessary amendments in future editions of the book.

Printed and bound in Spain by Edelvives

2010 2009 2008 2007 2006
10 9 8 7 6 5 4 3 2